QUEST Program I

Social Skills Curriculum for Elementary School Students with Autism

Ready-to-use lessons with games,
role-play activities, and more!

QUEST Program I was developed by

JoEllen Cumpata, MA, CCC
Speech and Language Pathologist

Susan Fell, LMSW
Student Assistance Specialist

QUEST Program I: Social Skills Curriculum for Elementary School Students with Autism

All marketing and publishing rights guaranteed to and reserved by

FUTURE HORIZONS INC.

721 W. Abram Street
Arlington, Texas 76013
800-489-0727
817-277-0727
817-277-2270 (fax)
E-mail: info@FHautism.com
www.FHautism.com

Printed in United States of America

ISBN: 9781941765043

To our students,
who continue to inspire us
with their wit, humor, and courage.

About the Authors

JoEllen Cumpata is currently a school-based Speech Language Pathologist (SLP). She was formerly a clinical supervisor at Michigan State University, teaching classes related to providing school-based speech and language services. JoEllen also served as a clinical SLP at Massachusetts General Hospital and Children's Hospital of Boston, working with adults and children. JoEllen has a Master's degree in Speech Language Pathology.

Susan Fell has been a school social worker for 15 years working primarily at the middle school level with students with autism, emotional, and cognitive impairments. Prior to that, Susan was a vocational counselor, youth employment coordinator, and parenting educator. She earned her Master's degree in Social Work from Arizona State University and her School Social Work Certification from Wayne State University in Detroit, Michigan.

The authors welcome your feedback! You can e-mail them at QUESTsocialskills@gmail.com.

Table of Contents

QUEST Program I: Social Skills Curriculum for Elementary School Students with Autism
© by JoEllen Cumpata and Susan Fell. Future Horizons, Inc.

Unit 4: Everybody Has Feelings **191**

All About QUEST Program I

The QUEST Program I Story

The QUEST Program I Primary Model was developed by a school social worker and speech language pathologist to address the needs of children who have social skills and pragmatic language challenges. The program applies an intensive proactive approach to teaching social skills, combining written instruction with games, activities and student interaction. The goal of the program is to help students gain a better understanding of human behavior and interaction, and to provide them with opportunities to become familiar with and comfortable using the social skills and pragmatic language necessary to be successful at school and in the community.

Students with social skills deficits benefit from regular instruction and practice in order to maximize the generalization of skills outside of the classroom. Unlike their peers, these students do not typically interpret social cues, nuances and rules of interaction, even when provided with an inclusive education in a general education setting. Often children with challenges in social skills become overwhelmed or anxious around their peers. QUEST Program I students learn about social skills through experiential stories, role-play, games, activities, discussions, friendly feedback from peers, and real-world experience.

Research Based Program

Social interaction difficulties often coexist with a variety of other language difficulties. QUEST Program I offers systematic instruction in social skill and pragmatic language development provided in a small group setting. Evidence indicates that "social skills group for school-aged children with ASD were considered an established" evidence-based practice.

(Reichow & Volkmar, National Center for Evidenced-Based Practice in Communication Disorders, 2010, page 161).

Pragmatics is sometimes called the heart of communication because it can facilitate the development and maintenance of interpersonal relationships. (Hyter, 2007). The QUEST program for primary students is a research-based curriculum developed to provide instruction in social language communication and pragmatics. Pragmatic language consists of three major communication skills: using language for different purposes (greeting, requesting), changing language depending upon the needs of the listener (speaking differently on the playground than in a classroom), and lastly, following rules for conversation (taking turns in conversation, staying on topic, and rephrasing when the listener has misunderstood. (ASHA, 2014).

Skills in social communication highly correlate with positive outcomes for students with ASD. (National Research Council, 2001.) Consequently, programs that facilitate growth in social interaction provide critical comprehensive education for students with ASD. (Laurent & Prizant, 2005). In addition, researchers Gresham, Sugai and Horner (2001) reported that "the ability to interact successfully with peers and significant others is one of the most important areas of students' development."

Studies suggest that primary school-aged children with Autism Spectrum Disorders (ASD) should receive instruction (individual and small group) tailored to the needs of the child. National Initiative for Autism: Screening and Assessment & Le Couteur, 2003). Experiential stories, role-play, and peer/adult feedback (Lord & McGee, 2001) using the QUEST curriculum are designed to meet these age-appropriate, individualized goals.

The QUEST Program I consists of structured teaching, with an emphasis on the physical organization of the setting, predictable schedules, and individualized use of teaching methods as suggested by the National Autism Center (2009). Units include topics such as communicating with others, having friends, and being safe.

Empirical data suggests that the most effective social skills training for students with developmental disabilities such as ASD incorporate modeling, coaching, and reinforcement systems. With these factors in mind, the QUEST curriculum was designed to teach the "hidden curriculum" and unwritten rules of social interaction. The program provides intensive, sequential instruction in an interactive format which appeals to students. The intensive nature of the program is supported by studies that suggest intervention should be provided in a repeated fashion. (January & Casey, et al., 2011).

Additionally, while generalization and maintenance have traditionally been the weak links in social skills training programs, they are considered crucial parts of this type of programming (Gresham et al. 2001, McConnell, 2002). The comprehensive nature of the QUEST Program I facilitates generalization and maintenance of skills.

Program Description

QUEST Program I consists of six units covering a variety of topics:

- Unit 1 - School Success (5-8 Topic Lessons)
- Unit 2 – Communicating with Others
- Unit 3 – Having Friends
- Unit 4 – Everybody Has Feelings
- Unit 5 – Being Safe
- Unit 6 – Being Responsible

Units are divided into five to eight topic lessons. Topics can be presented at home with parents or other family members, or in small groups or classroom settings. The program was designed to be co-taught in a school setting, but it can be adapted for use by parents, therapists, or others.

Each topic lesson is presented during a three-day or three-class cycle; however, activity days can be lengthened or modified as needed. Day one provides students with basic information about the skill by reading and discussing a story. Day two gives students the opportunity to practice the skill through individual and group activities, including investigation, observation, group projects, games, and role-play. Day three reinforces learning as students complete a fill-in-the blank report and/or play a board game to increase their comfort level with the skill. Students are reminded and expected to use learned skills during subsequent lessons.

It is highly recommended that QUEST Program I students meet two to three times per week for approximately 45 minutes. Group size is most effective when limited to eight or fewer students. Facilitators utilize a predictable schedule, visual reminders, regular prompts and feedback regarding learned skills, and reinforcements to maximize learning. Students benefit from working in a team while learning about behaviors, demonstrating understanding, and practicing in a safe environment. Weekly updates with suggestions for continued practice at home are provided to parents. Skill generalization is evaluated by both parents and teachers upon completion of each unit.

Weekly Schedule

Following a predictable weekly schedule helps reduce student anxiety. An organized class-room with a supply closet containing individual student QUEST Program I binders, mate-rials, and snacks is helpful. Students are expected to report to class on time and complete check-in procedures daily. These procedures can be varied, but typically include gathering materials and writing the day's topic in a planner. Colorful "QUEST Program I Rules and Procedures" posters and daily activity reminder cards are displayed in the classroom to help students remember procedures and successfully meet expectations. The date and current topic should also be written clearly on the board.

Stories

Stories introduce the concepts involved in skills development and give examples of ways students should, and also should NOT perform the skill. To increase understanding in a group setting, facilitators should ask one student to read a paragraph aloud and ask members of the group 'wh' questions about that paragraph. Students can also be asked to summarize the paragraph by putting it into their own words. Time is often spent discussing a paragraph before continuing with the reading. Examples from the students' own experiences can also be shared if applicable to help the students understand the skill and how it impacts their school day.

Activities

Each story is supported by one or more activities. Procedures and materials needed are described on the activity sheets. Activities may involve role-play, use of scenario cards, story-telling, or handouts. Activity sheets can be shown on a whiteboard or made into reusable activity sheets with poster board.

Materials for each activity are included and can be copied on colored paper or card stock before use. It is recommended that they be laminated if possible for ease of reuse, and some materials may need to be enlarged and placed on poster board if used in a group setting. Encouraging students to move about, role-play, or interact during activities increases interest and learning.

Activities are designed to help students become comfortable with skills and generalize learning. Each may be repeated throughout the year and facilitators and parents should encourage continued skill use.

Group Fill In the Blank Reports or Review Game

To further increase learning, students can play the topic Review Game or can be placed in small groups consisting of two to three students to complete and then present a Fill In the Blank Report. After each presentation, peers should give compliments and suggestions to presenters to increase presentation quality, while teaching additional skills of accepting criticism and observing others.

Reinforcement

Students with social and pragmatic language skill deficits may not understand the importance or need for social skill instruction and practice. Often these students are unaware of their deficits and may be reluctant to participate in the program. Providing incentives is one way to encourage participation. Additionally, students benefit from feedback from teachers, facilitators, parents, and peers.

Incentive guidelines are presented to students during the first week of class. Tickets, tokens, or coupons can be used as a motivational tool to encourage students to complete basic classroom procedures. Criteria for earning incentives should be concrete and achievable. Suggested criteria include arriving to class on time, completing check-in procedures, and participating in discussions or activities. Tokens can also be combined for group-earned activities such as a movie or pizza day.

Parent Support

Gaining parent and academic team support is essential to the program's success. Parent updates provide parents with information and suggestions to assist them in continuing to practice at home. Sample Parent Updates, fliers, evaluations, and additional information are included for your use.

Parent Updates

QUEST Program I Parent Updates are designed to enable parents to continue skill building at home with their child. Each experiential story can be supported with a Parent Update, which can be e-mailed or sent home to parents. Specific guidelines are given in each update to assist parents in understanding what skill has been taught, as well as specific rules or vocabulary used to support the skill, and ways to practice at home.

Student Evaluation

Student evaluations can be provided to parents, teachers, or others to determine if skills are becoming generalized. Evaluation can also be used as a pre/post assessment.

Unit Descriptions

Unit 1 –School Success

1-1 Paying Attention

1-2 Staying in My Seat

1-3 Listening and Waiting My Turn

1-4 Following Directions

1-5 School Work and Homework

1-6 Asking for Help

1-7 Doing My Best and Making Mistakes

Unit 2 – Communicating with Others

2-1 Greetings

2-2 Talking with Others

2-3 Talking without Words

2-4 Keeping a Conversation Going

2-5 Asking Questions

2-6 Ending a Talk

Unit 3 - Having Friends

Unit 4 – Everybody Has Feelings

Unit 5 – Being Safe

Unit 6 – Being Responsible

QUEST Program I: Social Skills Curriculum for Elementary School Students with Autism
© by JoEllen Cumpata and Susan Fell. Future Horizons, Inc.

Sample Correspondence, Reports, and Forms

Form 1   Teacher Introductory Flier – to present program to teachers and other administrative and support staff.

Form 2   Parent Introductory Letter – to inform parents when their child has been identified as a possible candidate for QUEST Program I.

Form 3a and b   Parent Introductory Flier (two samples provided) – to present program to parents of students who may be eligible for participation in the program or for students already enrolled.

Form 4   QUEST Program I Parent/Teacher Evaluation – to inform parents and teachers of skills recently learned and gain feedback on generalization of skills.

Form 5   QUEST Program I Rules and Procedures (3 pages) - visual reminder to display in the classroom.

Form 6a, b, and c   Daily Reminders Cards – visual reminders to display in the classroom.

Form 7   Successful Student Game – can be played after each skill is taught and practiced.

Questioning, Understanding, and Exploring Social Skills and Pragmatic Language Together (QUEST)

QUEST Program I is now available for students who may benefit from direct instruction and support for improving social and pragmatic language skills. Students participate two to three days per week. The class is facilitated by a teacher, speech pathologist, school social worker, or psychologist. Parent permission is required.

The goals of QUEST Program I are to improve student social and pragmatic language skills through the use of experiential stories, small group work, role-play, games, activities, and regular practice. Units include:

- School Success
- Communicating with Others
- Having Friends

- Everybody Has Feelings
- Being Safe
- Being Responsible

Parents are given suggestions on ways they can assist in reinforcing and maintaining skill development. Teachers and parents may also be asked to provide monthly feedback regarding progress.

If you have questions or would like a program facilitator to share information with parents and the team at the next IEP, please complete the form attached and return to _____ _____.

QUEST Program I Student Nomination Form

Student Name _____ Grade_____

Nominator's Name/Phone_____

Next IEP Date _____ School_____

(School Letterhead)

(Date)

Dear (parent name),

(School name) currently offers the QUEST Program I for students who may benefit from additional opportunities during the school day to learn about and practice social interaction and nonverbal communication. Your child has been identified as someone who may gain valuable skills from participation in this program.

Classes meet two to three days per week. Students participate in a small group setting and have opportunities for hands-on practice, role-play, and other experiential activities designed to increase their proficiency and comfort with appropriate social skills.

Enclosed you will find a flier describing the program. Please contact your child's special education teacher if you have questions or wish to discuss the program in detail.

Sincerely,

Welcome to Student QUEST Program I

Students Questioning, Understanding, and Exploring Social Skills and Pragmatic Language Together

Your student is scheduled to participate in the Student QUEST Program I this year.

- The goals of this program are to improve student social interaction and communication skills through the use of experiential stories, small group work, role-play, hands-on activities, and regular practice.

- Students meet in a small group setting two to three days each week.

- Please find a list of the topics we will be covering this year.

- Weekly updates will be e-mailed to parents with helpful suggestions on ways you can support your child's success.

The Student QUEST facilitators are:

_____

_____

_____

QUEST Program I

Questioning, Understanding, and Exploring Social Skills and Pragmatic Language Together

Does your child need additional support to ...

- make and keep friends?

- interpret body language and other social cues?

- manage emotions and handle stress?

If so, they may benefit from participation in QUEST Program I

- The goals of this program are to improve student social interaction and communication skills through the use of experiential stories, small group work, role-play, hands-on activities, and regular practice.

- Students meet in a small group setting two to three times per week.

- Weekly updates are e-mailed to parents, and provide helpful suggestions on ways to maintain and build skills at home.

- QUEST Program I is offered for _____ grade students with more in-depth study and advanced topics presented to second and third-year participants. Units include:

  1. School Success

  2. Communicating with Others

  3. Having Friends

  4. Everybody Has Feelings

  5. Being Safe

  6. Being Responsible

For more information contact: _____

QUEST Program I Parent/Teacher Evaluation

Student Name _____ Date _____

Parent/Teacher Name _____

The past several weeks in QUEST Program I we have been focusing on

_____

Please complete the rating scale below to assist us in determining how well the student listed above has generalized the skills taught. Check boxes which identify how often you have observed the skills listed during the past few weeks.

Skill	Does Independently	Does Only With Adult Reminders	Improvement Noted (Post-test only)

Comments_____

_____

Thank you for your input!

Classroom Rules and Procedures

Students participating in QUEST Program I are expected to follow standard rules and procedures. Rules help students feel comfortable and help teachers maintain an efficient classroom.

1. Come to QUEST Program I on time.

2. Come to QUEST Program I without complaining.

3. Complete "check-in" procedures.

    - Get a pencil

    - Get your binder

    - Have a seat

4. Participate in daily activities.

    - Pay attention

    - Answer questions

    - Complete activities

Story Day

Learn

QUEST Program I: Social Skills Curriculum for Elementary School Students with Autism
© by JoEllen Cumpata and Susan Fell. Future Horizons, Inc.

Activity Day

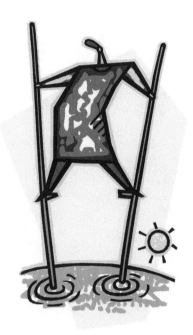

Practice

Report Day

Share

QUEST Program I Successful Student Game

Directions - Enlarge pieces on brightly colored paper, cut out, and paste on poster board, as shown in sample below. Laminate.

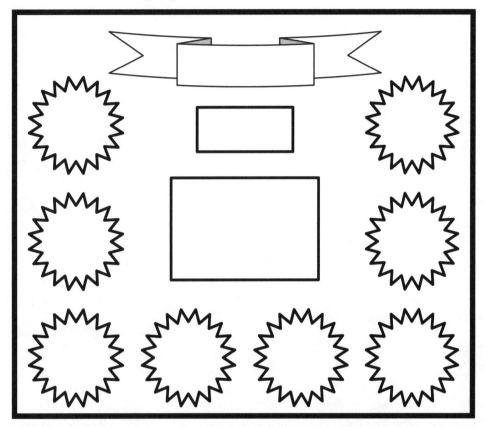

The skill we are learning about is …	**QUEST Successful Student Game Rules** 1. The teacher goes first. 2. Play goes to the right. 3. Write skill in the center. 4. Roll dice. 5. Act or tell what is written on star. 6. Try your best, and be a good sport.

QUEST Student Success Game

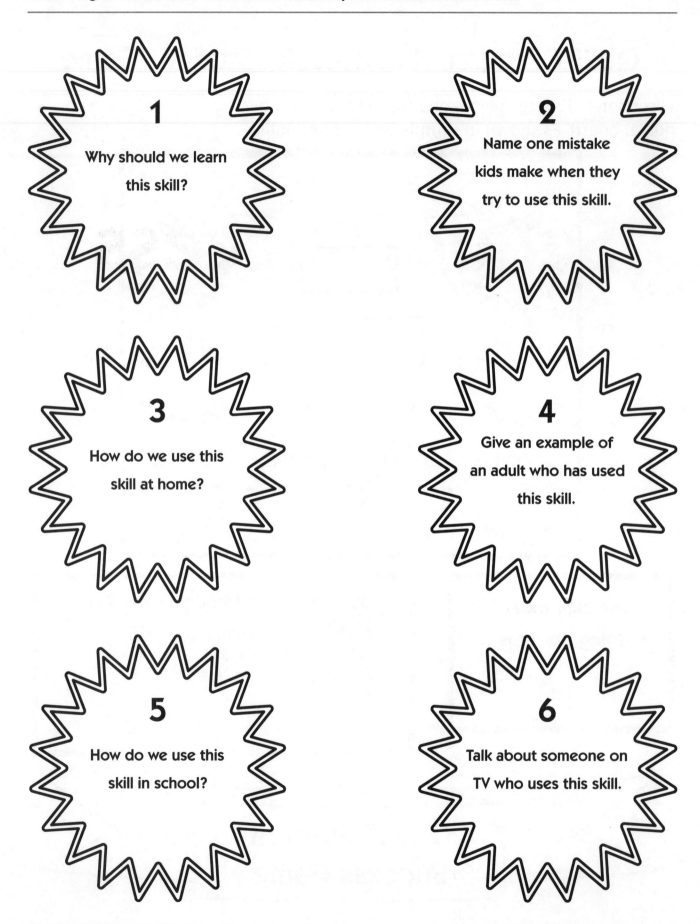

1 Why should we learn this skill?

2 Name one mistake kids make when they try to use this skill.

3 How do we use this skill at home?

4 Give an example of an adult who has used this skill.

5 How do we use this skill in school?

6 Talk about someone on TV who uses this skill.

Unit 1

School Success

Goals and Objectives Unit 1 - School Success

Goals

To learn and practice basic skills needed to function successfully in elementary school.

Objectives

➢ To understand why paying attention is important and practice four simple steps to pay attention.

➢ To appreciate staying seated and learn when it is appropriate to request to move about in class.

➢ To gain an appreciation of turn-taking when speaking.

➢ To learn about the purpose for school work and homework, and practice ways to tolerate boredom.

➢ To understand when it is appropriate to ask for help in class and practice effective ways to ask for help.

➢ To tolerate errors in self and others, and gain an appreciation for achieving personal best.

Stories, Activities, and Parent Updates

Stories can be read by parents, teachers, or students. Often students gain a deeper understanding of skills when stories are discussed in detail in a group setting. Asking students to summarize paragraphs, relate their personal experiences, and complete activities are all effective ways to increase generalization of skills. Parent Updates provide additional ways to continue learning at home.

Topics included in this unit are:

1. Paying Attention

2. Staying in My Seat

3. Listening and Waiting My Turn

4. Following Directions

5. School Work and Homework

6. Asking for Help

7. Doing My Best and Making Mistakes

Paying Attention - Story 1-1

All kids need to learn new things. Kids can learn new things at home. Parents, grandparents, aunts and uncles can teach kids new things. Sisters and brothers can teach kids new things. Kids learn new things on their computer and on the TV. Kids can learn new things in school too.

In order to learn, kids need to listen. In order to learn, kids need to look at the person who is talking. Listening and looking at the person talking is called PAYING ATTENTION. When kids pay attention, it means that they are watching closely and listening, so that they can learn.

If kids put their head down, they are not paying attention. If kids talk when someone else is talking, they are not paying attention. If kids play with their books, pencils, or school supplies when the teacher is talking, they are not paying attention.

Teachers, parents, and friends like it when we pay attention to them. When we are paying attention, we can learn. When people think we are paying attention, they know we care about what they are talking about.

I want to learn in school. I want people to know I care about learning. I can try to pay attention to teachers, parents, and friends when they are talking to me. When I pay attention, I will look, listen, and sit still. When I pay attention I can learn.

Paying Attention - Activity Sheet 1-1

Name _____

1. Find these words or phrases in the story and highlight them:

   learn   listen   sit still

   teach   closely   look

2. Circle the things we should do when we are paying attention. Put an 'X' over the things we should NOT do when we are trying to pay attention.

   Look at the person talking   Lay our head down

   Keep our back straight   Look out the window

   Keep our hands still   Play with our pencil

   Tap our foot   Hum a tune

Paying Attention - Activity Sheet 1-1

Materials –

- Paying Attention story

- Two small plastic containers (approximately 5"x 5")

- Happy Teacher/Unhappy Teacher cards

- Paying Attention/Not Paying Attention scenario cards

Procedure –

- Prior to class, cut out scenario cards.

- Read "Paying Attention" story aloud in class and discuss.

- Display two containers, one each labeled with "Happy Teacher/Unhappy Teacher" cards.

- Place "Paying Attention/Not Paying Attention" scenario cards on table.

- Ask a student to select a scenario card, read it silently, and then act out the behavior.

- Ask the group if the behavior is an example of paying attention or an example of not paying attention.

- Ask the student to place the card in the appropriate container which reflects how a teacher might feel about a behavior.

- Continue until all students have had a turn.

Happy Teacher/Unhappy Teacher - Cards 1-1

Happy Teacher

Unhappy Teacher

Paying Attention/Not Paying Attention - Scenario Cards 1-1

Lay your head on the desk.	Look at the ceiling.
Tap your pencil on the desk loudly.	Get up and walk around the room.
Talk loudly to the person next to you.	Look at the floor and pick your fingernails.
Look out the window.	Bounce both of your legs up and down.

Paying Attention/Not Paying Attention - Scenario Cards 1-1

Sit up straight in
your chair.

Look at the
teacher's face.

Put both of your
hands in your lap.

Keep your hands and
feet still.

Look at the teacher's
face and yawn.

Look at the teacher's
face and smile.

Whisper to the
person next to you.

Laugh out loud.

Paying Attention/Not Paying Attention - Activity Sheet 1-1

Materials –

- Paying Attention story

- Paying Attention/Not Paying Attention heading cards

- Large sheets of blank paper for each student (art paper, poster board or 18"x14" or 11"x17" paper)

- Magazines

- Pencils

- Scissors

- Glue sticks

Procedure –

- Prior to class, copy "Paying Attention/Not Paying Attention" heading cards, one each per student.

- Read "Paying Attention" story aloud to class.

- Provide each student with magazines, scissors, glue, and poster board or large sheet of paper.

- Ask students to divide their paper in half and glue a Paying Attention card on one half, Not Paying Attention card on the other half.

- Ask students to browse through the magazines and cut out pictures which show people paying attention and not paying attention.

- Have students make a collage of these pictures by gluing them to the poster board in the appropriate section.

- Ask the students to select a few examples from their collage to share with the group.

- Discuss how students knew a person was paying attention or not paying attention.

Paying Attention/Not Paying Attention - Heading Cards 1-1

Paying Attention

Not Paying Attention

Paying Attention - Report 1-1

Names_____

Date_____

Directions: Read the sentences below. Fill in the blanks for each question. Look at the story or use the word box if you need help.

1. All kids need to learn _____ things.

2. Kids can learn new things at home from parents, _____, aunts and uncles, or even sisters and brothers

3. Kids all can learn new things in _____ too.

4. In order to learn, kids need to _____.

5. In order to learn, kids need to _____ at the person who is talking.

6. Listening and looking at the person taking is called _____ _____.

7. If kids put their _____ down or talk when someone else is talking, they are not paying attention.

Paying Attention - Report 1-1

8. If kids _____ with their books, pencils, or school supplies when the teacher is talking, they are not paying attention.

9. When we are paying attention we can_____.

WORD BOX

look	play	grandparents
paying attention	school	head
learn	listen	new

QUEST Program I Social Skills Curriculum for Elementary School Students with Autism
© by JoEllen Cumpata and Susan Fell. Future Horizons, Inc.

QUEST Program I UPDATE!

Dear Parent,

Your child has been working hard in QUEST Program I this week to learn and practice social skills. The story we read to introduce our new skill was called:

Paying Attention

Together we have learned:

- Why students must pay attention when others are talking.

- How it looks when students pay attention.

You can help your child practice at home by:

- Modeling attentive listening at home by looking at your child when he/she is talking.

- Encouraging your child to use these strategies for paying attention when others are talking at home:

  1. Look at the person talking.
  2. Keep our hands and feet still.
  3. Listen and don't talk.

- Noticing times when your child is paying attention to others and giving them positive reinforcement.

  e.g., "Grandpa had a lot to say today, but I noticed you looked at his face the whole time. He knew you were listening."

  "You sat so still when your coach was giving directions! I bet you learned a lot!"

Thanks for your help!

Staying in My Seat - Story 1-2

Sometimes in class kids need to stay in their seats, listen, and be quiet. Other times, kids learn in class by moving around, working on a computer, talking, or doing things.

The teacher will usually tell kids when they need to stay in their seats and when they can get up and move around. Usually, kids need to stay in their seats when the teacher is talking about rules, showing how to do something, or giving important information.

Sometimes it is hard to sit for a long time. Sometimes when kids are supposed to stay in their seats, they want to get up. Some want to use the bathroom, some want to talk to other kids, or touch things in the room. Other kids just like to move around a lot.

If kids want to get up, they should quietly raise their hand and wait until the teacher calls on them. When the teacher calls on them, they can explain why they want to get up.

The teacher decides when it is okay for kids to move around. If a teacher says it is not a good time to get up, kids must stay in their seat.

 I can try to stay in my seat when my teacher is showing us how to do something or giving information. If I want to get up, I will raise my hand and wait for the teacher to call on me. This is what all kids need to do at school.

Staying in My Seat - Activity Sheet 1-2

Name _____

1. Find these words or phrases in the story and highlight them:

   quiet   stay   listen

   seats   raise   teacher

2. Look at the pictures below. Talk about which kids need to stay seated and which kids can move around.

Staying in My Seat - Report 1-2

Names_____

Date_____

Directions: Read the sentences below. Fill in the blanks for each question. Look at the story or use the word box if you need help.

1. Sometimes in class kids need to stay in their _____, listen, and be quiet.

2. Other times, kids learn in class by _____ around, working on a computer, talking, or doing other things.

3. The _____ will usually tell kids when they need to stay in their seats and when they can get up and move around.

4. Usually, kids need to stay in their seats when the teacher is talking about rules, showing how to do something, or giving important_____.

5. Sometimes it is _____ to sit for a long time.

6. Sometimes when kids are supposed to stay in their seats, they _____to get up to use the bathroom.

7. If kids want to get up, they should quietly _____ their hand and wait until the teacher calls on them, so they can explain why they want to get up.

8. The teacher _____ when it is okay for kids to move around.

9. If a teacher says it is not a good time to get up, kids must _____ in their seat.

WORD BOX

raise	moving	stay
seats	information	want
teacher	hard	decides

QUEST Program I UPDATE!

Dear Parent,

Your child has been working hard in QUEST Program I this week to learn and practice social skills. The story we read to introduce our new skill was called:

Staying in My Seat

Together we have learned:

- Students should usually stay seated at school.
- The teacher decides when students can move around.
- What to do if you feel you must move about during listening time.

You can help your child practice at home by:

- Scheduling regular weekly family times when your child is expected to stay seated and listen to adults. Good times for this are during meal conversations or weekly family meetings.

- Begin with short seated periods during these times and extend as the child gets older.

- Notice when your child has stayed seated and praise them.

    e.g., "Boy, that sure was a long speech your Cub Scout leader made today. I know it was hard for you to sit that whole time. You did a really good job."

Thanks for your help!

QUEST Program I Social Skills Curriculum for Elementary School Students with Autism
© by JoEllen Cumpata and Susan Fell. Future Horizons, Inc.

Listening and Waiting My Turn - Story 1-3

School is a place where people take turns talking and listening. Students learn best this way. Waiting and taking turns means that everyone who has something to say will get a chance to say it.

Usually when teachers, adults, or kids are talking, they don't want others to interrupt. Talking when someone else is talking is called interrupting. When people interrupt, others may think they don't care about what is being said, or that they are being rude. Being interrupted usually makes other people angry.

If the teacher is talking, students should wait to talk or ask questions until the teacher stops talking. Sometimes a teacher will ask "Does anyone have any questions or comments?" This means it is a good time to ask questions or say something about what the teacher has said. It is not the time to talk about other things.

If you are talking with kids, you should wait until they pause and then say what you want to say. Usually kids say one or two sentences, and then wait for others to talk.

Sometimes, kids forget to take turns and interrupt their friends or teachers. This is frustrating and can make others angry. If a student interrupts someone, it is best to stop talking, apologize for interrupting, and let the other person finish with what they have to say.

Teachers and other students like it when we listen to them and take turns talking. This is the best way to learn and make friends. I can try to be a good listener and wait until it is my turn to talk. I can try to talk about the same things my teacher or friends are talking about. I should apologize when I interrupt.

Listening and Waiting My Turn - Activity Sheet 1-3

```
F  O  V  S  E  R  P  I  L  J  K  Y  C  T  A  C
H  W  M  W  X  S  B  V  I  A  P  M  T  Z  E  I
M  R  A  F  S  V  H  U  S  M  W  X  A  A  W  D
C  X  A  I  W  C  M  K  T  L  K  N  K  B  G  R
V  B  L  W  T  A  X  W  E  C  B  L  E  A  R  N
P  J  N  V  C  X  S  C  N  A  G  H  T  I  K  L
O  I  I  T  P  B  N  W  S  X  C  J  U  L  M  T
B  S  E  I  O  L  L  O  N  Z  Y  R  R  B  U  Y
N  D  J  T  G  W  I  F  E  T  G  U  N  H  E  U
U  G  I  N  T  E  R  R  U  P  T  S  S  T  A  P
E  I  T  P  N  H  L  J  V  D  V  J  O  P  N  E
L  R  E  Y  C  V  X  N  U  E  K  S  E  L  G  D
S  U  L  E  H  U  H  O  Z  L  I  E  O  L  R  Y
E  D  D  V  J  R  B  N  A  X  B  F  U  P  Y  N
T  E  I  B  C  S  Z  T  C  U  L  Y  W  E  B  I
R  O  L  R  O  E  J  V  N  Z  I  O  T  T  E  R
```

Find and circle these words and phrases

Interrupt	Wait	Talk	Learn
Take turns	Angry	Listen	Rude

Answer Key

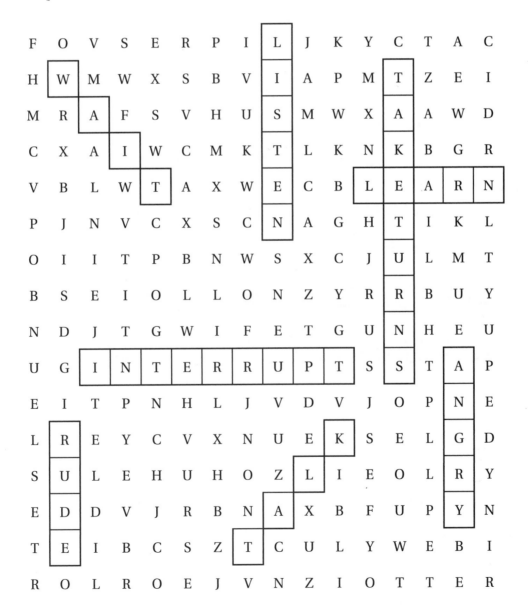

Listening and Waiting My Turn - Report 1-3

Names_____

Date _____

Directions: Read the sentences below. Fill in the blanks for each question. Look at the story or use the word box if you need help.

1. School is a place where people take _____ talking and listening.

2. Waiting and taking turns means that _____ who has something to say will get a chance to say it.

3. Usually when teachers, adults, or kids are talking they don't want others to _____.

4. Interrupting is _____ when someone else is talking.

5. Being interrupted usually makes other people _____.

6. If the teacher is talking, students should _____to talk or ask questions until the teacher stops talking.

7. If you are talking with kids, you should say _____ or _____ sentences, and then wait for others to talk.

8. If we interrupt someone, it is best to stop talking, _____
for interrupting, and let the other person finish with what they
have to say.

WORD BOX		
one	interrupt	turns
everyone	angry	two
apologize	wait	talking

QUEST Program I UPDATE!

Dear Parent,

Your child has been working hard in QUEST Program I this week to learn and practice social skills. The story we read to introduce our new skill was called:

Listening and Waiting My Turn

Together we have learned:

- In school, students take turns talking and listening.

- The definition of interrupting.

- It is important to stop talking and apologize when we interrupt.

You can help your child practice at home by:

- Model both good listening and interrupting for your child. When you interrupt, as we all do from time to time, stop and apologize to your child.

- Remind your child about listening and waiting to speak:

  e.g., "Jeremy, I've got something important to talk with you about. I really want you to try to remember to listen and wait your turn to talk."

- Notice when your child has been a patient listener.

  e.g., "Wow, Dad sure had a lot to say this morning. I know it was hard for you to listen without interrupting, but you sure did a good job."

Thanks for your help!

Following Directions - Story 1-4

Everybody needs to follow directions. In school, kids need to follow the teacher's directions.

Teachers ask students to do a lot of things. Teachers ask students to:

- Get out school supplies
- Complete school work
- Take turns
- Work with other students
- Be quiet
- Go to another class, to lunch, or home for the day

When kids follow the teacher's directions, they can learn. When kids follow the teacher's directions, they will get a good grade. When kids follow the teacher's directions, they will be safe.

At home it is important to follow directions too. Parents, grandparents, and other people who take care of kids give directions.

Parents ask kids to do a lot of things. Some things parents ask kids to do are:

- Take a shower
- Help with chores
- Do your homework
- Go to bed
- Get ready for school

When we follow directions at home we will be safe. When we follow directions at home we will get homework and chores done. When we follow directions at home our parents are happy.

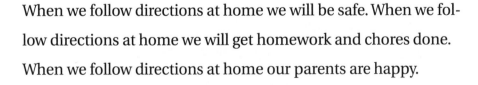

Following Directions - Activity Sheet 1-4

Names_____

Date _____

1. Find these words or phrases in the story and highlight them:

directions	happy	teachers
learn	safe	quiet

2. Tell a story about one of the pictures below. Is the student in the picture following directions or not?

QUEST Program I Social Skills Curriculum for Elementary School Students with Autism
© by JoEllen Cumpata and Susan Fell. Future Horizons, Inc.

3. Circle the things we should do when we follow directions at school. Put an 'X' through the things we should NOT do when we try to follow directions.

shout   get out our school supplies

complete our school work   take turns

lay our head down   punch another student

tear our paper   be quiet

listen to the teacher   throw things

4. When you are done with your activity follow these directions:

   a. Put your activity sheet in the 'Activity' section of your QUEST Program I binder;

   b. Put your QUEST Program I binder away;

   c. Sit back in your seat and raise your hand.

Following Directions - Report 1-4

Names_____

Date_____

Directions: Read the sentences below. Fill in the blanks for each question. Look at the story or use the word box if you need help.

1. Students need to follow the teacher's _____ in school.

2. Teachers ask _____ to do a lot of things.

3. Teachers might ask students to:

    a. Get out _____ _____.

    b. Complete school work.

    c. Take turns.

    d. Be _____.

4. When kids _____ the teacher's directions, they can learn.

5. When kids follow the teacher's directions, they will get a _____ grade.

QUEST Program I Social Skills Curriculum for Elementary School Students with Autism
© by JoEllen Cumpata and Susan Fell. Future Horizons, Inc.

6. When kids follow the teacher's directions, they will be _____.

7. At home, it is important to follow your _____ directions too.

8. Parents ask kids to take a shower, help with chores, do _____, go to bed, and get ready for school.

9. When we follow directions at home our parents are _____.

WORD BOX

happy	good	safe
directions	homework	parents'
school supplies	students	follow
quiet		

QUEST Program I UPDATE!

Dear Parent,

Your child has been working hard in QUEST Program I this week to learn and practice social skills. The story we read to introduce our new skill was called:

Following Directions

Together we have learned:

- Everyone needs to follow directions.

- When we follow directions, we will learn, get better grades, and be safe.

You can help your child practice at home by:

- Prompting your child before giving directions.

  e.g., "Emily, I'm going to give you some directions that are very important, so pay attention."

- Give directions one at a time OR use a visual reminder schedule with directions listed.

- Let your child know when you are pleased that they followed all the directions.

  e.g., "That was a long list of things to do, but I'm so happy you really listened."

Thanks for your help!

School Work and Homework - Story 1-5

Students have to do work when they are in school. Teachers and parents like it when kids do their work. Doing work helps students learn.

It's important to look at the teacher and listen to the directions the teacher gives. This helps kids understand what to do. Some kids write down things to remind them of what they need to do. Kids should do their work and turn it in when the teacher tells them to, even when it is boring or hard.

Sometimes work is done in school and sometimes it has to be done at home. Sometimes work is easy or fun to do. Other times work is hard or even boring. It is important to try to do a good job even when the work is hard or boring.

When homework is hard or boring, it helps to do it first and save fun work for later. Sometimes kids can ask a grown up for help with hard work.

Teachers and parents like it when we do our work. We learn new information and get better grades when we do our work.

I can try to listen to the directions, do my work, and turn in it when the teacher says I should. I can try to do hard or boring work before I do other fun tasks. I can get help from an adult or work as part of a student group. Completing my work, even my hard or boring work, will make me a successful student!

School Work and Homework - Activity Sheet 1-5

Name _____

1. Find these words or phrases in the story and highlight them:

   work   learn   boring

   hard   grades   information

2. Circle the three subjects that are the easiest for you below:

School Work and Homework - Activity Sheet 1-5

Materials –

- School Work and Homework story

- School Work and Homework game board

- School Work and Homework Happy Face/Frowning Face game pieces

- School Work and Homework scenario cards

Procedure –

- Assemble "School Work and Homework" game prior to class, cut out game pieces, and scenario cards.

- Read "School Work and Homework" story aloud in class and discuss.

- Lay "School Work and Homework" game board on top of the table and ask students to gather around.

- Place "School Work and Homework" scenario cards face down in the box in the center of the game board.

- Give each student four to five happy faces and four to five frowning faces game pieces.

- Explain to students that students always have choices about doing work. Explain that some choices are positive and help us to complete work; others are negative and keep us from completing work.

- Select one of the scenario cards from the perimeter of the game and read aloud to the group.

- Read each choice space on the game board aloud.

- Ask the group which choice space represents the best choice. Place a smiling face game piece on this space.

- Ask the group which choice space represents a negative choice. Place a frowning face game piece on this space.

- Discuss.

- Allow each student a turn.

School Work and Homework - Game Board 1-5

Directions - Enlarge pieces on brightly colored paper and paste on poster board, as shown in sample. Laminate.

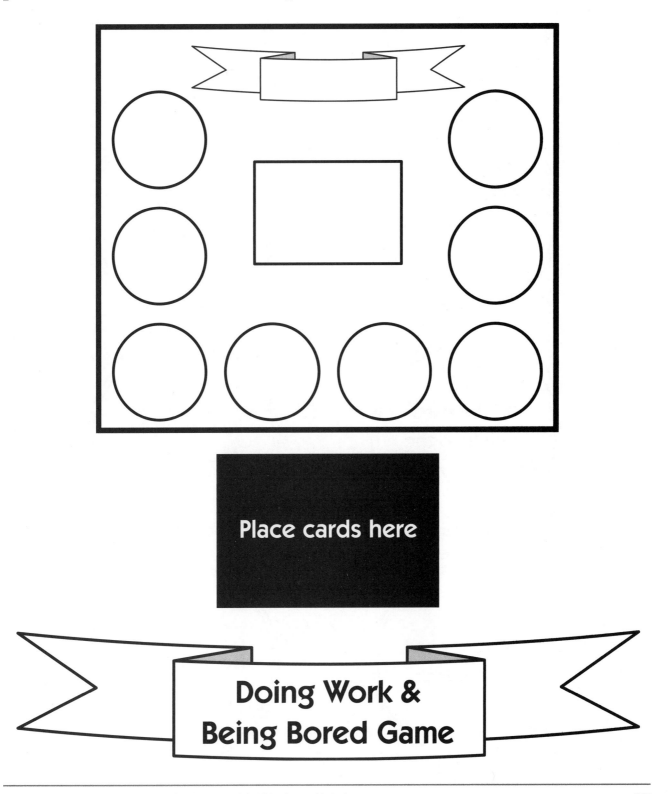

Do something else.

Ask an adult for help.

Ask another student for help.

Don't do the work.

Do the hard work first, the fun work next.

Complain to the teacher.

Lay your head on the desk.

Do your best.

QUEST Program I Social Skills Curriculum for Elementary School Students with Autism
© by JoEllen Cumpata and Susan Fell. Future Horizons, Inc.

School Work and Homework Smiling Face - Game Pieces 1-5

School Work and Homework Frowning Face - Game Pieces 1-5

QUEST Program I Social Skills Curriculum for Elementary School Students with Autism

School Work and Homework - Scenario Cards 1-5

Your teacher asks you to do your math problems. You really enjoy doing math.

The class is supposed to read quietly. The book is really boring.

You need to finish your social studies map, but you don't like coloring.

The class is working on a science project, but you are confused.

You are supposed to play soccer in gym, but you can't kick the ball right.

You are writing a story about dogs, but you don't like dogs.

In music, the class is practicing a song for the concert. You can't sing very well.

Everyone is picking a book in the library. You don't know what book to pick.

School Work and Homework - Scenario Cards 1-5

Your teacher asks the class to read their books outside. You would rather stay inside.

You are supposed to work on a book report on the computer. You would rather play a computer game.

You have reading and science homework. You like science better.

Your teacher says "You can read your book or work on your art project." You don't like reading.

You are making Valentine's cards in class. You think they are really stupid.

The math problems are too hard.

You are supposed to find an interesting picture in a magazine, none look interesting.

The science project you are working on is really fun.

QUEST Program I Social Skills Curriculum for Elementary School Students with Autism
© by JoEllen Cumpata and Susan Fell. Future Horizons, Inc.

School Work and Homework - Report 1-5

Names_____

Date_____

Directions: Read the sentences below. Fill in the blanks for each question. Look at the story or use the word box if you need help.

1. Students have to do work when they are in _____.

2. Teachers and _____ like it when kids do their work.

3. It's important to look at the teacher and _____ to the directions, so kids will understand what to do.

4. Some kids _____ _____ things to remind them of what they need to do.

5. Kids should do their work and turn it in when the teacher tells them to, even when it is _____ or hard.

6. Sometimes work is done in school and sometimes it has to be done at _____.

7. It is _____ to try to do a good job even when the work is hard or boring.

8. When homework is hard or boring it helps to do it
   _____ and save fun work for later.

9. Sometimes kids can ask a grown up for _____ with
   hard work.

10. We learn new information and get better _____ when we
    do our work.

WORD BOX

help	home	listen
write down	first	important
boring	school	grades
parents		

QUEST Program I UPDATE!

Dear Parent,

Your child has been working hard in QUEST Program I this week to learn and practice social skills. The story we read to introduce our new skill was called:

School Work and Homework

Together we have learned:

- Why school work and homework are important.

- How to ask for help when work is hard.

- Why students must do work, even if it is boring or difficult.

You can help your child practice at home by:

- Avoiding arguments regarding work completion when your child complains by:

  1. Acknowledging that school and homework are not always fun or interesting.

  2. Stating that while they may not always be fun, assignments are required.

  3. Working closely with your child's teacher, school social worker, or psychologist to develop a homework plan if consistent problems arise.

- Encouraging your child to complete tedious, difficult, or boring work first, and save more interesting or fun work for last.

- Praising your child when they complete work.

Thanks for your help!

Asking for Help - Story 1-6

Students are learning new information all of the time. Some teachers talk very fast. Some teachers don't give enough information. Some teachers are hard to understand. Sometimes, kids can get confused about what they are supposed to do.

When kids don't know what to do, they should ask their teacher for help. It's easy to forget what to do. Kids might need more information to do a good job. All kids have questions. It's a good idea to ask for help when kids have questions.

Teachers know that kids have questions. All teachers are ready to answer questions, but some teachers get upset when questions are asked at the wrong time or in the wrong way.

When kids have questions about the lesson, they should:

- Wait until the teacher has stopped talking.
- Raise their hand.
- When the teacher calls on them, ask their question.
- Say "Thank you" after the teacher has answered their question.

Kids can do their work and get good grades when they have all of their questions answered. Teachers like to answer questions when they are asked in the right way and at the right time. I will try to ask for help in the right way when I have a question. I will try to wait until the right time to ask my question.

Asking For Help - Activity Sheet 1-6

Name _____

1. Find these words or phrases in the story and highlight them:

   questions   information   ask

   raise   help   forget

2. The pictures below show students who might need help. Tell a story about why they need help and how they should ask for it.

Asking for Help - Activity Sheet 1-6

Materials –

- Asking for Help story

- Asking for Help table game

- Asking for Help scenario cards

Procedure –

- Prior to class, cut out "Asking for Help" scenario cards.

- Read "Asking for Help" story aloud in class and discuss.

- Lay "Asking for Help" table game on top of the table and ask students to gather around.

- Place "Asking for Help" scenario cards face down in the boxes on the perimeter of the game board.

- Explain to students that there are times to ask for help and other times to wait. Also explain that there are good ways and not so good ways to ask for help.

- Select one of the scenario cards from the perimeter of the game and read aloud to the group.

- Ask the group if they think the student on the card did a good job of asking for help or a poor job.

- Place on appropriate box in the center of the game.

- Allow each student a turn.

Asking for Help - Game Board 1-6

Asking for Help - Scenario Cards 1-6

Your locker won't open.

You feel like you are going to throw up.

A student pushes you in the hall.

A student calls you "stupid face."

You are cutting something and the scissors are too big.

You are coloring a picture and you need a blue crayon.

You are hungry, but it is not lunch time yet.

You don't like what your mother put in your lunch.

QUEST Program I Social Skills Curriculum for Elementary School Students with Autism
© by JoEllen Cumpata and Susan Fell. Future Horizons, Inc.

Asking for Help - Scenario Cards 1-6

The teacher is talking too fast.	The teacher is too loud.
The teacher asks the class to sit down. Someone is in your seat.	Your pencil breaks.
You fall and cut your knee on the playground.	You don't remember what class you have next.
Your nose is running, but you don't see any tissue.	You don't understand what your teacher wants you to do.

Asking for Help - Scenario Cards 1-6

You don't know how to spell a word.

You can't figure out how to add two numbers.

The student next to you keeps whispering when the teacher is talking.

You're not sure what your homework is.

You are taking a test and you don't understand a question.

You've been raising your hand for a while, but your teacher doesn't see you.

You are working with a group of students and they are doing the wrong thing.

You need to use the bathroom really bad, but the teacher is talking to someone.

QUEST Program I Social Skills Curriculum for Elementary School Students with Autism

Asking for Help - Report 1-6

Names_____

Date_____

Directions: Read the sentences below. Fill in the blanks for each question. Look at the story or use the word box if you need help.

1. Students are learning new_____ all of the time.

2. Some teachers talk very _____, don't give enough information, or are hard to understand.

3. Sometimes, kids can get _____ about what they are supposed to do.

4. When kids don't know what to do, they should ask the _____.

5. It's easy to _____ what to do, or need more information to do a good job.

6. It's a good idea to _____ for help when kids have questions.

7. All teachers are ready to answer _____, but some teachers get upset when questions are asked at the wrong time or in the wrong way.

8. When kids have questions about the lesson, they should:

- Wait until the teacher has stopped _____.

- Raise their hand.

- When the teacher calls on them, ask their question.

- Say _____ _____ after the teacher has answered their question.

WORD BOX

forget	confused	ask
teacher	information	talking
thank you	questions	fast

QUEST Program I UPDATE!

Dear Parent,

Your child has been working hard in QUEST Program I this week to learn and practice social skills. The story we read to introduce our new skill was called:

Asking for Help

Together we have learned:

- Why it is important to ask for help when confused or in need of additional information.

- When it's an appropriate time to ask for help.

- How to ask for help in a polite way.

You can help your child practice at home by:

- Encouraging your child to ask for help when they are confused.

- Reminding your child of the appropriate way to ask for help at home.

  e.g., "Emily, I know you are frustrated because you don't know how to start the new computer, but I was talking with Grandma on the phone. Next time I will expect you to wait until I'm off the phone to ask for help."

- Referring your child to helpful people rather than answering all their questions.

  e.g., "Nick, I think the librarian could probably help you find the right book."
  "Why don't you ask your teacher about this assignment tomorrow? I'm not sure I understand the directions."

Thanks for your help!

Doing My Best and Making Mistakes - Story 1-7

Most kids like to get good grades, but sometimes they don't feel like doing their best. Sometimes it is really hard to do your best.

It's hard to do your best when work is boring or confusing. It's hard to do your best when you feel sick or tired. It's hard to do your best when you don't feel like being at school.

Sometimes doing your best is hard, but teachers and parents like kids to try their best. Kids get better grades when they do all the work assigned and try their best. Teachers know students are trying their best when they:

- Pay attention.

- Listen carefully.

- Ask questions.

- Do their work.

Sometimes even when kids try their best, they still make mistakes. Making mistakes is okay. All people—even teachers and parents—sometimes make mistakes. When kids make mistakes, it is their teacher's job to help. This is all part of school.

When kids make a mistake, it is smart to ask for help and try again. This is how students learn. I can get good grades when I try to do my best work. If I make a mistake, it's smart to ask the teacher for help and try again.

Doing My Best and Making Mistakes - Activity Sheet 1-7

Name _____

1. Find these words or phrases in the story and highlight them:

   work   confusing   mistakes

   smart   try   again

2. Pretend you are a teacher and correct all the spelling and grammar mistakes in the paragraph below. Then pretend your teacher is the student who wrote the paragraph, and tell them about their mistakes in a friendly and helpful way.

Sometimes even wen kids try their best thay stil make misstakes. making mistakes is okay. All people, even techers And parents, sometimes make mistakes. Wen kids make mistakes it istheir teacher's job to halp. this is all part of scool

Doing My Best and Making Mistakes - Report 1-7

Names_____

Date_____

Directions: Read the sentences below. Fill in the blanks for each question. Look at the story or use the word box if you need help.

1. Most kids like to get good _____.

2. But sometimes it is really hard to do your _____.

3. It's _____ to do your best when work is boring or confusing, or when you feel sick or tired.

4. Sometimes doing your best is hard but_____ and parents like kids to try their best.

5. Teachers know students are trying their best when they:

    a. Pay _____.

    b. _____ carefully.

    c. Ask questions.

    d. Do their _____.

QUEST Program I Social Skills Curriculum for Elementary School Students with Autism
© by JoEllen Cumpata and Susan Fell. Future Horizons, Inc.

6. Making mistakes is _____.

7. When kids make a _____, it is smart to ask for help and try again. This is how students learn.

WORD BOX

attention	okay	work
mistake	best	hard
teachers	Listen	grades

QUEST Program I UPDATE!

Dear Parent,

Your child has been working hard in QUEST Program I this week to learn and practice social skills. The story we read to introduce our new skill was called:

Doing My Best and Making Mistakes

Together we have learned:

- Why it's important for students to try their best in school.

- It is normal for students to sometimes feel work is too hard or boring.

- What students should do if they feel work is too hard or boring.

- Student mistakes are common and teachers are there to help.

You can help your child practice at home by:

- Asking your child to share one example of their best work each week.

- Praising your child when they persevere through difficult or boring assignments.

- Modeling the appropriate way to accept criticism.

  e.g., "Today I made a big mistake at work. Mr. Smith showed me how to correct it though and I really thanked him. I won't make that kind of mistake again."
  "Brian, can you show me how to log on to this computer program again? It seems like I'm making some kind of mistake."

Thanks for your help!

QUEST Program I Parent/Teacher Evaluation Unit 1 - School Success

Student Name _____ Date _____

Parent/Teacher Name _____

The past several weeks in QUEST Program I we have been focusing on School Success. Please complete the rating scale below to assist us in determining how well the student has generalized the skills taught. Check boxes which identify how often you have observed the skills listed during the past few weeks.

Skill	Does Independently	Does Only With Adult Reminders	Improvement Noted (Post-test only)
Paying Attention: Listening to others, using good eye contact, sitting up, and keeping hands and feet still while listening.			
Staying in My Seat: Remaining seated during class, meals, family events or other functions.			
Listening and Waiting My Turn: Allowing others to participate in conversation or other forms of turn-taking, keeping interruptions to a minimum, and apologizing when interrupting others.			
Schoolwork and Home Work: Attempting homework, asking for help from adults when needed, trying difficult work before more enjoyable tasks.			
Asking for Help: Waiting until others are done talking to request assistance, and saying "Thank you" when provided assistance.			
Doing My Best and Making Mistakes: Attempting difficult or boring homework, sharing an example of their best work weekly, accepting criticism and correction without argument.			

Comments_____

Thank you for your input!

Unit 2

Communicating with Others

Goals and Objectives Unit 2 - Communicating With Others

Goals

To learn and practice basic communication skills.

Objectives

➢ To understand why we use greetings and appropriate greetings for school and home.

➢ To appreciate social conversation and learn appropriate topics and methods to use when talking with peers.

➢ To recognize body language and the ways in which additional information is given and shared through facial expressions, gestures, and voice tone.

➢ To be aware of the need for turn-taking when speaking.

➢ To learn useful ways to ask questions in class and during friendly conversation.

➢ To identify when and how to end a conversation.

Stories, Activities, and Parent Updates

Stories can be read by parents, teachers, or students. Often students gain a deeper understanding of skills when stories are discussed in detail in a group setting. Asking students to summarize paragraphs, relate their personal experiences, and complete activities are all effective ways to increase generalization of skills. Parent Updates provide additional ways to continue learning at home.

Topics included in this unit are:

1. Greetings

2. Talking with Others

3. Talking without Words

4. Keeping a Conversation Going

5. Asking Questions

6. Ending a Talk

Greetings - Story 2-1

It is nice to be friendly. When kids go to school, they are supposed to be friendly. One way to be friendly is by using a greeting, like saying "Hello."

At home, I can use a greeting. I can say "Hello" to my family. I can say "Hello" when I wake up in the morning. I can say "Hello" when I come home from school. I can say "Hello" when people come to my house.

When I say "Hello" to my family, it is okay to give them a hug or a kiss. Hugs and kisses are special greetings only for the people we love. It is **NOT** okay to hug or kiss friends or teachers at school. I only hug and kiss my family.

At school, I can be friendly by using greetings. I can say "Hello" to my friends and teachers. I can say "Hello" when I come into class. I can say "Hello" when I see friends at lunch. When I say "Hello" at school I should:

1. Stand in front of the person.
2. Wait until they are not talking.
3. Smile.
4. Say "Hello."

I can be friendly when I use a greeting. I can say "Hello" to my family. I can say "Hello" to my friends. I can be friendly.

Greetings - Activity Sheet 2-1

Name _____

1. Find these words or phrases in the story and highlight them:

   hello   family   friendly

   hug   greeting   lunch

2. Prior to class, cut out "Greetings" game cards. Play the "Greetings" game. Turn the "Greetings" game cards upside down on the table. Let each student choose a card and show how they would greet the person on the card. Talk about their greeting.

   • Did they give the correct greeting?

   • Were there other greetings they could have used?

Greetings - Game Cards 2-1

How do I greet Grandma?

How do I greet Grandpa?

How do I greet Mom?

How do I greet Dad?

How do I greet someone at a party?

How do I greet my uncle
at Thanksgiving?

QUEST Program I Social Skills Curriculum for Elementary School Students with Autism
© by JoEllen Cumpata and Susan Fell. Future Horizons, Inc.

Greetings - Game Cards 2-1

How do I greet my doctor?

How do I greet Santa?

How do I greet the mail carrier?

How do I greet trick-or-treaters?

How do I greet another student who I like?

How do I greet someone at church?

Greetings - Game Cards 2-1

How do I greet my friend?

How do I greet a baby?

How do I greet someone in the library?

How do I greet my sister?

How do I greet someone on the bus?

How do I greet my teacher?

Greetings - Game Cards 2-1

How do I greet my brother?

How do I greet a dog?

How do I greet my cousin?

How do I greet my aunt?

Greetings - Report 2-1

Names_____

Date_____

Directions: Read the sentences below. Fill in the blanks for each question. Look at the story or use the word box if you need help.

1. It is nice to be _____.

2. One way to be friendly at school is by using a _____ like saying "Hello."

3. At home, I can say "Hello" to my _____.

4. I can say "Hello" when I wake up in the _____, when I come home from school, or when people come to my house.

5. When I say "Hello" to my family, it is okay to give them a _____ or a kiss because these are special greetings only for the people we love.

6. I only hug and kiss my family, so it is NOT okay to hug or kiss friends or teachers at _____.

7. At school, I can say _____ to my friends and teachers.

8. I can say "Hello" when I come into _____ or when I see friends at lunch.

9. When I say "Hello" at school, I should:

   a. Stand in _____ of the person;

   b. Wait until they are not talking;

   c. Smile;

   d. Say "Hello."

WORD BOX

morning	front	class
hug	friendly	greeting
family	school	"hello"

QUEST Program I UPDATE!

Dear Parent,

Your child has been working hard in QUEST Program I this week to learn and practice social skills. The story we read to introduce our new skill was called:

Greetings

Together we have learned:

- That using personal greetings is a way to be friendly.

- When we greet someone, we should:

  - Stand in front of the person;
  - Wait until they are not talking;
  - Smile and use a greeting.

- That we only use hugs and kisses with family members and people we love.

You can help your child practice at home by:

- Using greetings.

- Reminding your child to greet others.

    e.g., "I see Dad just came home—run and give him a hug."

    "Don't forget to say 'Hello' when we see your coach at the game today."

Thanks for your help!

QUEST Program I Social Skills Curriculum for Elementary School Students with Autism
© by JoEllen Cumpata and Susan Fell. Future Horizons, Inc.

Talking with Others - Story 2-2

Kids like to talk to other kids. Kids like to talk with their parents. Kids like to talk to teachers too. Talking to other people is called having a conversation. Having a conversation is fun and interesting.

When kids talk to each other, they should talk about what they both like. When kids talk to each other, they could talk about school. When kids talk to each other, they can talk about TV shows, video games, or music. When kids talk to each other, they can talk about their pets or their family.

When kids talk to other kids, they need to:

1. Stand at arm's length away;

2. Look at the person's face;

3. Use a greeting like "Hi."

It can be fun and interesting to talk to other kids. When I talk to kids, I can stand at arm's length away. When I talk to kids, I can look at them and say "Hi". When I talk to other kids, I should talk about things we both like. Having a conversation is fun.

Talking with Others - Activity Sheet 2-2

Name _____

1. Find these words or phrases in the story and highlight them:

    talk   greeting   interesting

    video games   conversation   look

2. What do kids talk about? Play the "Name A Topic" game. Go around the group and see how many things you can name to talk about.

   Here are a few ideas to get you started.

   • Pets
   • TV shows
   • Video games

3. Choose a picture and tell a story about the kids talking to each other.

4. Put this list in the right order by putting a number by the sentence. Put a number 1 by the thing you should do first. Put a number 2 by the thing you should do next. Look back at your story for help.

_____ Say "Bye."

_____ Say something they might be interested in.

_____ Stand at arm's length away from the person.

_____ Smile and say "Hi".

_____ Look at the person's face.

_____ Wait for them to say something back to you.

Talking with Others - Report 2-2

Names_____

Date   _____

Directions: Read the sentences below. Fill in the blanks for each question. Look at the story or use the word box if you need help.

1. Kids like to talk to _____ kids.

2. Talking to other people is called having a _____.

3. Having a conversation is _____ and interesting.

4. When kids talk to each other, they can talk about TV shows, _____ _____, or music.

5. When kids talk to other kids, they need to:

   a. _____ at arm's length away;

   b. Look at the person's _____;

   c. Use a _____ like "Hi."

6. When I talk to other kids, I should talk about things we _____ like.

7. _____ a conversation is fun.

QUEST Program I Social Skills Curriculum for Elementary School Students with Autism
© by JoEllen Cumpata and Susan Fell. Future Horizons, Inc.

WORD BOX

fun	Having	Stand
face	other	both
video games	greeting	conversation

QUEST Program I UPDATE!

Dear Parent,

Your child has been working hard in QUEST Program I this week to learn and practice social skills. The story we read to introduce our new skill was called:

Talking with Others

Together we have learned:

- Having a conversation can be fun and interesting.

- When we talk to other people, we should do the following:

  Stand at arm's length away;

  Look at the person's face;

  Use a greeting, like "Hi."

- When we want to have a conversation, we need to talk about things others are interested in.

You can help your child practice at home by:

- Having daily conversations.

- Encouraging and reminding your child about good conversation skills.

  e.g., "I really liked how you waited until I was done talking and then told me what you thought."
  "I know you really like to talk about trains, but when Bobby comes over, he might want to talk about baseball, too."

Thanks for your help!

Talking without Words - Story 2-3

Kids can talk with other kids by using words. Kids can talk to adults by using words. Kids can even talk to their pets by using words. When we talk using words, we give information.

We can also give information without talking or using words. Sometimes when we tell or show people something, we do it without using words. Communicating without using words is called body language.

Kids can talk with body language when they:

- Move their body like waving, shrugging their shoulders, or stomping their feet.
- Move their face like frowning or smiling.

When kids talk to other kids, it's also important that they look at the other kid's body language. Paying attention to see if kids are smiling or frowning lets you know how they are feeling. When kids look at you, they might want to talk to you. When kids walk away, they probably don't want to talk to you.

Another way kids can give information is by showing how they feel. One way kids show how they feel is by using a loud or soft voice. Loud talking tells people we are angry, excited, or really want to be heard. Soft talking tells people we are sad, lonely, or don't want everyone to hear.

Kids should pay close attention to how other kids move their faces and bodies. Kids should listen to how loud or soft other kids are talking. Paying attention tells us a lot about how other kids feel. When I try to pay close attention, I can understand people better.

Talking without Words - Activity Sheet 2-3

Name _____

1. Find these words or phrases in the story and highlight them:

   communicating   attention   body language

   words   understand   voice

2. The pictures below show students talking without words. Tell a story about one of the pictures below.

3. Prior to class, cut out "Talking Without Words" cards. Play the "Talking Without Words" game. Pick a card and read it out loud. Choose one student to act it out.

Talking without Words - Cards 2-3

Without using words, show how you would look if you got an "A" on your test.

Without using words, show how you would look if you broke the teacher's vase.

Without using words, show how you would look if your dog was sick.

Without using words, show how you would look if you won a race.

Without using words, show how you would look if you wanted the teacher to call on you.

Without using words, show how you would look if your science teacher brought a lizard to class.

Without using words, show how you would look if you were paying attention.

Without using words, show how you would look if you were bored.

Talking without Words - Cards 2-3

Without using words, show how you would look if you couldn't go on a field trip.

Without using words, show how you would look if you lost your lunch.

Without using words, show how you would look if you were picked for the team.

Without using words, show how you would look if you fell in the hall.

Without using words, show how you would look if you said "Hello" to a friend in the library.

Without using words, show how you would look if you wanted others to be quiet.

Without using words, show how you would look if you wanted to greet a friend who was standing very far away.

Without using words, show how you would look if you had a headache.

Talking without Words - Cards 2-3

Without using words, show how you would look if you were getting a new puppy.

Without using words, show how you would look if you heard the fire alarm at school.

Talking without Words - Report 2-3

Names_____

Date_____

Directions: Read the sentences below. Fill in the blanks for each question. Look at the story or use the word box if you need help.

1. Kids _____in many ways.

2. Kids can talk with other kids by using _____.

3. Communicating without words is called using _____ _____.

4. Kids can communicate without using words when they move their body by waving, _____ their shoulders, or stomping their feet.

5. Kids can communicate without using words when they move their face by frowning or _____.

6. Another way kids can show how they _____ is by using a loud or soft voice.

7. _____ talking tells people we are angry or excited.

8. Soft talking tells people we are _____ or lonely.

9. Kids should pay close _____ to how other kids move their face and body.

WORD BOX

feel	shrugging	sad
Loud	smiling	words
attention	body language	communicate

QUEST Program I UPDATE!

Dear Parent,

Your child has been working hard in QUEST Program I this week to learn and practice social skills. The story we read to introduce our new skill was called:

Talking without Words

Together we have learned:

- We can give information or talk without words—this is called body language.

- Watching for body language and facial expressions gives us more information.

You can help your child practice at home by:

- Noticing body language and helping your child to understand its meaning.

    e.g., "I'm guessing you don't like our dinner plans, since you've put your head down and are frowning. Am I right?"
    "If you watch your cousin very closely, you will be able to tell if he really likes his birthday gift because he will smile and maybe even jump up and down."

- Trying to predict body language with your child.

    e.g., "When your Dad finds out about the car, how do you think his face will look?"

Thanks for your help!

Keeping a Conversation Going - Story 2-4

Kids like to have conversations. Having a conversation is fun and interesting. It can be fun to talk to kids and have a conversation. Sometimes talking to kids is easy. Sometimes talking to kids is hard. Sometimes it's hard to know what to say when I have a conversation.

When I talk with kids, I need to think of what I want to say to them. Usually kids talk to other kids about things they are both interested in. Kids talk about school. Kids talk about pets. Kids talk about their family. Kids can talk about movies, TV shows, video games, and other fun things.

Some kids talk too much! Some kids don't talk very much at all. When kids have a conversation, it is important that they both do some talking and listening. The conversation needs to go back and forth.

When kids have a conversation, they have to think for a few moments before they talk. When kids have a conversation, they should think about who they want to talk with, what the other kid likes, and what to talk about.

When kids talk to other kids, they need to:

1. Stand at arm's length away;
2. Look at the person's face;
3. Use a greeting, like "Hi."

When kids talk, they can say things or ask questions. They should wait to listen to what the other kids say. Talking is like playing the game of ping-pong. Talking goes back and forth like the ping-pong ball goes back and forth. Most talking goes back and forth for about two or three sentences then it might be time to end the conversation.

It can be fun to talk to other kids. When I talk to other kids, I need to talk about things we both like. When I talk to other kids, I need to listen.

Keeping a Conversation Going - Activity Sheet 2-4

Name _____

1. Find these words or phrases in the story and highlight them:

   school   kids   ping-pong

   talk   back and forth   conversation

2. List two things you could talk to other kids about:_____
   _____
   _____
   _____

3. Choose a picture and tell a story about what the kids might say to keep the conversation going.

Keeping a Conversation Going - Report 2-4

Names_____

Date _____

Directions: Read the sentences below. Fill in the blanks for each question. Look at the story or use the word box if you need help.

1. Kids like to have a _____.

2. Having a conversation is _____ and interesting.

3. Sometimes it's hard to know what to _____ when I have a conversation.

4. Usually kids talk to other kids about things they are both _____ in.

5. Kids can talk about movies, TV shows, _____ and other fun things.

6. Some kids talk too _____. Some kids don't talk very much at all.

7. When kids have a conversation, it is important that they _____ do some talking.

8. It is important that they do some _____.

9. A conversation needs to go _____ and forth.

WORD BOX

listening	say	back
fun	conversation	much
video games	interested	both

QUEST Program I Social Skills Curriculum for Elementary School Students with Autism
© by JoEllen Cumpata and Susan Fell. Future Horizons, Inc.

QUEST Program I UPDATE!

Dear Parent,

Your child has been working hard in QUEST Program I this week to learn and practice social skills. The story we read to introduce our new skill was called:

Keeping a Conversation Going

Together we have learned:

- Conversations can only keep going if each person does some talking and listening.

- Conversations happen when people talk about something they are both interested in.

You can help your child practice at home by:

- Helping to direct conversation with your child.

    e.g., "I know your sister had her big speech today. Why don't you ask her how it went when she gets home?"

    "You've been talking a lot about your dinosaur book, but I'm not as interested in it as you are. What could we talk about that we both like?"

Thanks for your help!

Asking Questions - Story 2-5

One way kids show they like other kids is by having a conversation with them. A conversation means talking together. Talking together is fun, but it is important to keep the talking going. One way to keep the talking going is by asking questions.

When you want to ask a question, you need to think about what you want to ask. Kids ask questions about other kids' classes. Kids ask questions about other kids' pets or their family. Kids ask questions about what other kids like. Most kids like video games, movies, or sports, so it is usually okay to talk about those things with kids.

If you want to ask a question, it is important that you wait until the other person is not talking. When they are not talking, you should look at their face, smile, and say their name. Then you can ask your question and wait for the person to answer.

Kids also ask questions in their classes. Kids ask their teachers questions about class work. Kids ask their teachers questions about homework. When you want to ask the teacher a question, you should make sure the teacher is done talking.

Then:

- Think about what question you want to ask.
- Raise your hand.
- Ask your question.
- Wait for the teacher to answer.

I can show I like other kids by asking them questions. I can get information from my teachers by asking them questions. It can be fun and helpful to ask questions.

QUEST Program I Social Skills Curriculum for Elementary School Students with Autism

Asking Questions - Activity Sheet 2-5

Name _____

1. Find these words or phrases in the story and highlight them:

   wait   conversation   kids

   question   teacher   information

2. Give an example of questions kids might ask:

   a. A question I might ask my teacher. _____

   _____

   b. A question I might ask my friend. _____

   _____

3. Choose a picture and tell a story about what questions you could ask this student to keep the conversation going.

Asking Questions - Report 2-5

Names_____

Date _____

Directions: Read the sentences below. Fill in the blanks for each question. Look at the story or use the word box if you need help.

1. One way kids show they are interested in other kids is by having a _____ with them.

2. To _____ a conversation going kids can ask each other questions.

3. When you want to ask a question you need to _____ about what you want to ask.

4. Kids ask questions about other kids' classes, pets, or their _____.

5. If you want to ask a question, it is important that you wait until the other student is not _____.

6. When they are not talking, you should look at their _____, smile, and say their name.

7. Then you can ask your question and _____ for the person to answer.

8. If kids want to ask their teacher a question, they should wait until the teacher is done talking and then _____ their hand.

9. I can show I am _____ in other kids by asking them questions.

WORD BOX

talking	keep	face
interested	think	wait
raise	conversations	family

QUEST Program I UPDATE!

Dear Parent,

Your child has been working hard in QUEST Program I this week to learn and practice social skills. The story we read to introduce our new skill was called:

Asking Questions

Together we have learned:

- One way to keep a conversation going is to ask questions related to what the other person is talking about.

- It is also important to ask questions about things you don't understand at school and home.

You can help your child practice at home by:

- Play the "Questions" game. When your child gets home from school, ask them a question about their day. Then tell them that they need to ask you a question. (Be sure the questions get more specific than the general, "How was your day?").

Thanks for your help!

Ending a Talk - Story 2-6

Kids like to talk to other kids. Kids usually talk for two or three minutes. Kids might say two or three sentences. After two or three minutes of talking, you might want to stop talking. You might need to go to class or get home. If you want to stop talking, you cannot just walk away. If you just walk away, kids might think you are mad or mean.

When you want to stop talking, you need to let the other kid know. You can let the other kid know by following these steps:

- Look at the other kid. Wait until they look at you.
- Use an exit line. Exit lines are words like: "See you later," "Bye," or "Have a good day."
- Wait for the other kid to say "Bye."
- Walk away.

When you follow these steps, it is okay to leave. This is how you end a conversation. When you end a conversation like this, kids will not think you are unfriendly. They will not think you are being mean. They will understand you need to stop talking and leave.

Ending a Talk - Activity Sheet 2-6

Name _____

1. Find the following words and phrase in the story and highlight them.

mean	exit line	unfriendly
kids	"Bye"	walk away

2. Read the sentence and then circle the right answer.

    a. An example of an exit line is "Bye."   T   F

    b. Most kids do not like to talk to other kids.   T   F

    c. You have to stop talking when you go to class.   T   F

    d. When the bell rings and class starts, you should keep talking with your friend.   T   F

    e. Kids might think you are mean if you forget to use an exit line and you just walk away.   T   F

3. Choose a picture and tell a story about the kids using an exit line.

Ending a Talk - Report - 2-6

Names_____

Date _____

Directions: Read the sentences below. Fill in the blanks for each question. Look at the story or use the word box if you need help.

1. Kids like to talk to other _____.

2. Kids usually talk for two or _____ minutes.

3. After two or three minutes of talking, you might want to _____ talking if you need to go to class.

4. If you want to stop talking, you cannot just _____.

5. If you just walk away, kids might _____ you are mad or mean.

6. When you want to stop talking, you can let the other kid know by following these steps:

    a. Look at the other kid. _____ until they look at you.

    b. Use an _____ _____. Exit lines are words like: "See you later," "Bye," or "Have a good day."

    c. Wait for the other kid to say _____.

    d. Walk away.

WORD BOX

wait	walk away	bye
kids	three	exit line
stop	think	

QUEST Program I UPDATE!

Dear Parent,

Your child has been working hard in QUEST Program I this week to learn and practice social skills. The story we read to introduce our new skill was called:

Ending a Talk

Together we have learned:

- A conversation cannot go on forever.

- We can use an exit line when we are ready to end a conversation.

You can help your child practice at home by:

- Use exit body language and words at home.

  e.g., "Well, I see it's getting close to 7:30. We'd better talk about this later and get to school."

- Remind your child about exit body language:

  e.g., "Did you notice that Grandpa kept looking at the TV when you were talking to him about your new video game? That probably means he was done talking about it and wanted to watch his show."
  "I saw Dad stand up and push his chair in after dinner when I was talking about our vacation. I guess he was done talking about it."

Thanks for your help!

QUEST Program I Parent/Teacher Evaluation
Unit 2 - Communication

Student Name _____ Date _____

Parent/Teacher Name _____

The past several weeks in QUEST Program I, we have been learning about communication. Please complete the rating scale below to assist us in determining how well the student has generalized the skills taught. Check the boxes that identify how often you have observed the skills listed during the past few weeks.

Skill	Does Independently	Does Only With Adult Reminders	Improvement Noted (Post-test only)
Greetings: Saying "Hello" to family, friends and at school. Hugging/kissing only family members.			
Talking with Others: Standing at arm's length away, looking at a person's face, using a greeting, and talking about topics others are interested in.			
Talking without Words: Using appropriate facial expressions/body language, recognizing body language of others, and responding correctly.			
Keeping a Conversation Going: Listening and talking during conversation, talking about topics others are interested in.			
Asking Questions: Asking related questions in conversation or in class listen and responding on topic to others' questions.			
Ending a Talk: Using exit lines ("Bye," "Gotta go," "See ya") before leaving a conversation.			

Comments_____

_____

Thank you for your input!

Unit 3

Having Friends

Goals and Objectives Unit 3 - Having Friends

Goals

To understand and practice appropriate peer social interaction.

Objectives

➢ To learn ways to approach peers on the playground.

➢ To understand and practice ways to join a peer group in play.

➢ To appreciate turn-taking.

➢ To learn appropriate times and places for humor and play, and improve their understanding and ability to engage in pretend play.

➢ To cope with losing at a game and to learn and practice the concept of good sportsmanship.

➢ To gain respect for personal choice in friendship, and learn ways to tolerate rejection.

➢ To develop resiliency when dealing with teasing and rough- play, and learn appropriate strategies for handling bullying.

Stories, Activities, and Parent Updates

Stories can be read by parents, teachers, or students. Often students gain a deeper understanding of skills when stories are discussed in detail in a group setting. Asking students to summarize paragraphs, relate their personal experiences, and complete activities are all effective ways to increase generalization of skills. Parent Updates provide additional ways to continue learning at home.

Topics included in this unit are:

1. Making Friends at School

2. Joining In

3. Taking Turns

4. Acting Silly

5. Winning, Losing and Being a Good Sport

6. Sharing Friends

7. Calling Friends on the Telephone

8. Dealing with Mean Kids

Making Friends at School - Story 3-1

Most students like to have friends at school. Friends can make the school day more fun and interesting. Friends talk about school subjects. Friends eat lunch together. Friends say "Hello" when they see each other in the hall.

Some kids have one or two friends, and some have more. Some kids have friends at school. Some kids have friends at home too. It is nice to have friends. It is nice to make new friends.

A good time to make friends at school is at lunch. The smart way to make new friends at lunch is to look for students we know. We might know kids from class. We might know kids from sports. We might know kids from our neighborhood.

To make a new friend, walk up to a student and:

- Stand at arm's length away;

- Smile;

- Say "Hi."

After friends say "Hi" to each other, they might talk about things they both like. Sometimes they will spend time with other kids and make more new friends.

I can meet new friends at school. When I have friends at school, my day will be more fun and interesting. At lunch I can walk up to students from my class, stand at arm's length away, smile, and say "Hi."

QUEST Program I Social Skills Curriculum for Elementary School Students with Autism
© by JoEllen Cumpata and Susan Fell. Future Horizons, Inc.

Making Friends at School - Activity Sheet 3-1

Name _____

1. Find these words or phrases in the story and highlight them:

   arm's length   neighborhood   students

   friends   smile   class

2. The pictures below show students making friends. Tell a story about one of the pictures below.

3. Circle the things we should do when we are trying to make new friends. Put an 'X' over the things we should NOT do when we are trying to make new friends.

Say bad things about them   Look at the person

Talk about things we both like   Pass gas

Smile   Say "Hi"

Pick your nose   Spend time together

Making Friends at School - Activity Sheet 3-1

Materials

- Making Friends at School story
- Making Friends at School Word Scramble poster
- Making Friends at School Word Scramble word cards
- Ten numbered envelopes
- Sticky poster tack

Procedure

- Prior to class, print two copies of the "Making Friends at School" - Word Scramble Answers, keep one copy for your records, and cut out the letters of each word from the other copy and place letters for each word in a numbered envelope.
- Read "Making Friends at School" story.
- Display "Making Friends at School" - Word Scramble poster in the room.
- Give each student a "Making Friends at School" - Word Scramble word card envelope.
- Ask students to dump the letters out of their envelope and make a word that relates to the story.
- When students have completed their word, ask the student with envelope number one to place his word on the correct space on the "Making Friends at School" - Word Scramble poster.
- Continue until all spaces are filled.
- For a simplified version, use a wipe-off marker to fill in some of the boxes on the poster using the correct letter(s).

Making Friends at School - Word Scramble
Poster 3-1

1. I can make new ☐☐☐☐☐☐ at school and have a fun and interesting day.

2. It is a good idea to have friends at ☐☐☐☐ and at school.

3. Friends make the day more ☐☐☐.

4. Friends at school can also make the day a lot more ☐☐☐☐☐☐☐☐☐☐.

5. ☐☐☐☐☐ is a good place to meet friends at school.

6. One smart way to decide who to say "Hi" to at lunch is to look for other kids from my ☐☐☐☐☐.

7. The first rule to remember when I want to make a friend on the playground is to stand at ☐☐☐'☐ length away.

8. Always remember to ☐☐☐☐☐ when you want to make a new friend.

9. When you are at arm's length away and have given your new friend a big smile, you can just say "☐☐."

10. After friends say "Hi," they sometimes ☐☐☐☐, play or just hang out together.

Making Friends at School - Word Scramble
Answers Activity 3-1

1. F R I E N D S

2. H O M E

3. F U N

4. I N T E R E S T I N G

5. L U N C H

6. C L A S S

7. A R M S

8. S M I L E

9. H I

10. T A L K

Making Friends at School - Report 3-1

Names_____

Date_____

Directions: Read the sentences below. Fill in the blanks for each question. Look at the story or use the word box if you need help.

1. Most students like to have _____ at school.

2. Friends can make the school day more fun and _____.

3. Friends talk about _____ subjects, eat lunch together, and say "Hello" when they see each other in the hall.

4. Some kids have one or two friends, and some have _____.

5. Some kids have friends at school. Some kids have friends at _____ too.

6. It is nice to have friends. It is nice to _____new friends.

7. One good time to make friends at school is at _____.

8. The smart way to make new friends at lunch is to look for _____ who we know.

9. We might know kids from _____, sports, or from our neighborhood.

10. To make a new friend, walk up to a student, stand at arm's length away, smile, and say "_____."

11. After friends say "Hi" to each other, they might talk about things they both _____.

```
┌─────────────────────────────────────────────────────────┐
│                     WORD BOX                             │
│                                                          │
│     "Hi"            make              friends            │
│                                                          │
│    students      interesting           more             │
│                                                          │
│     lunch           home               like             │
│                                                          │
│     school          class                               │
│                                                          │
└─────────────────────────────────────────────────────────┘
```

QUEST Program I UPDATE!

Dear Parent,

Your child has been working hard in QUEST Program I this week to learn and practice social skills. The story we read to introduce our new skill was called:

Making Friends at School

Together we have learned:

- Why friends are important.

- Where to make a new friend at school.

- Three steps to use to make a new friend.

You can help your child practice at home by:

- Encouraging your child to seek out friendships at home or at family events.

    e.g., "Jack, I know you are really enjoying your computer game, but your cousin Jesse is sitting all alone in the living room. Could you go and say "Hi" to him for me? He might be interested in seeing your aquarium."

- Reminding them of the three steps when meeting friends or family members:

    1. Stand at arm's length away;
    2. Smile;
    3. Say "Hi."

Thanks for your help!

Joining In - Story 3-2

Friends like to talk and hang out together. Friends talk together in the halls. Friends walk to class together. Friends hang out at lunch and after school.

Joining a group is like meeting a new friend. One good way to join a group is to:

- Walk up to the group;

- Stand at arm's length away;

- Smile;

- Say "Hi."

It is smart to watch the other kids in a group and listen to them, to see what to do next. If the group is talking, it is smart to talk about the same thing. Then the other kids know you are interested in joining the group.

Sometimes it is NOT a good time to join a group. If kids are already playing a game with teams, or talking about something private it may be a bad time to join the group. Sometimes kids might say "Go away." or "Leave us alone." These are also not good times to try to join a group.

Kids can make new friends when they join a group. If I want to join a group, I can walk up to the group, stand at arm's length away, smile, and say "Hi." I can decide if it is a good time to join a group. If it's not a good time, I can find other kids to hang out with.

Joining In - Activity Sheet 3-2

Name _____

1. Find these words or phrases in the story and highlight them:

   together   group   teams

   join   smile   friends

2. Circle the things we should do when we want to join in with a group. Put an 'X' over the things we should NOT do when we want to join in with a group.

   Yell if the group isn't listening to you.   Walk up to the group.

   Stand at arm's length away.   Smile.

   Talk about things the other kids are not talking about.   Hit the person talking if they won't listen to you.

   Say "Hi."   Try to talk to kids when the teacher is talking.

Joining In - Activity Sheet 3-2

Materials

- Joining In story

- Joining In scenario cards

- Joining In table game

Procedure

- Prior to class, cut out the "Joining In" scenario cards.

- Read "Joining In" story aloud in class and discuss.

- Lay "Joining In" table game on top of the table and ask students to gather around.

- Explain to students that there are good times to try to join in a group and other times that might not be the best choice.

- Select one of the scenario cards from the perimeter of the game and read aloud to the group.

- Ask the group if they think this would be a good time to join a group or not.

- Place on appropriate box in the center of the game.

- Allow each student a turn.

Joining In - Table Board Game 3-2

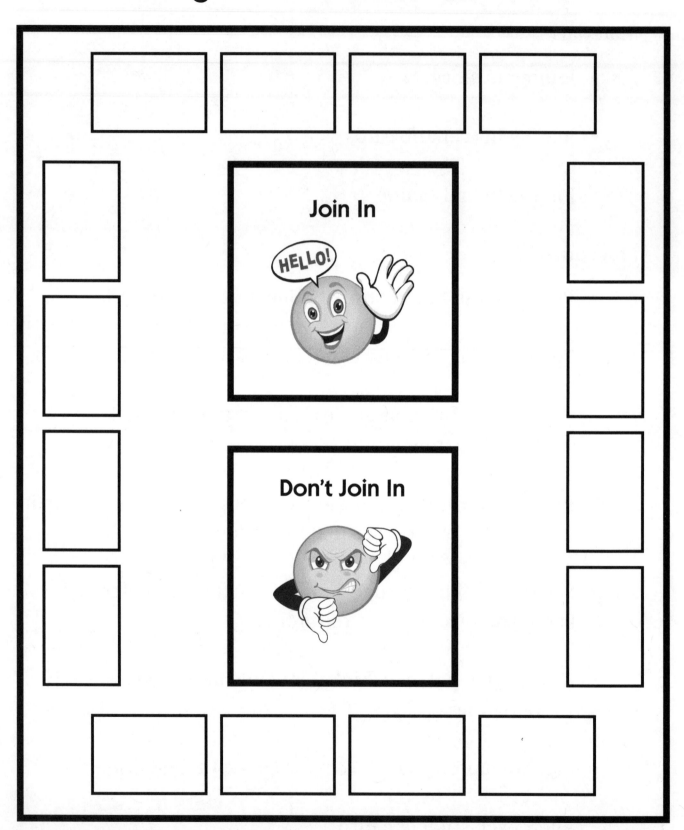

Joining In - Scenario Cards 3-2

You see three kids from your class throwing a ball on the playground.

One girl from your class is swinging on the swings.

Four teachers are talking near the school entrance.

The principal is talking to a child who is crying.

Four boys from your class are having lunch. There is an empty seat near them.

Two students are arguing over a jump rope on the playground.

Several students are having relay races on the playground.

You are walking down the hall with your class and you see another teacher showing her class a lizard.

Joining In - Scenario Cards 3-2

Four students are swinging on the jungle gym.

Two teams are playing football.

Two students from your class are walking home from school in front of you.

A group of parents are talking at a lunch table.

Two students are fighting on the playground.

Three kids from your class are working together on a project in art.

You see two students playing together after they have completed their work. You are still finishing work.

After school, several students are shooting basketballs on the playground. You are very good at basketball.

Joining In - Scenario Cards 3-2

The teacher has selected groups for a project. You want to be in another group.

You are walking near a group of students and one turns and says, "Leave us alone."

One girl from your class is sitting alone on a bench on the playground.

Your PE teacher asks for volunteers for a group game.

Four students are playing tag on the playground.

Three kids from your class are sitting under a tree talking at lunch.

Several students are playing four square on the blacktop.

A group of girls and boys are playing kickball on the playground. You have never played before.

Is It Okay to Join In Now? - Activity Sheet 3-2

Materials

- Joining In story

- Joining In poster

- Joining In scenario cards

Procedure

- Read "Joining In" story aloud in class and discuss.

- Display "It's Easy to Join In" poster and remind students of the steps.

- Place "Joining In" scenario cards face down on table.

- Explain that each student will select a scenario card, read it, decide if this is an appropriate time to join in and try to use the three joining in steps to act out what is on the card.

- Explain to the students that you, the classroom assistant, another adult, and student will pretend to be the other people described on each card.

- Discuss.

It's Easy to Join In! - Poster 3-2

If you want to join in remember to:

Stand at arm's length away

Smile

Use a greeting

Joining In - Report 3-2

Names_____

Date_____

Directions: Read the sentences below. Fill in the blanks for each question. Look at the story or use the word box if you need help.

1. Friends like to talk and _____ _____ together.

2. Friends talk _____ in the halls.

3. Friends walk to class together, hang out at _____ and after school.

4. Joining a group is like meeting a new _____.

5. One good way to join a group is to:

   Walk up to the _____.

   a. Stand one arm's length away;

   b. Smile;

   c. Say "Hi."

6. It is smart to watch the other kids in a group and _____ to them, to see what to do next.

7. If the group is talking, it is smart to talk about the _____ thing.

8. Then the other kids know you are _____ in joining the group.

9. Sometimes it is NOT a good time to join a group, like when kids are already playing a game with _____, or they say "Go away."

WORD BOX

group	teams	hang out
interested	together	same
lunch	listen	friend

QUEST Program I UPDATE!

Dear Parent,

Your child has been working hard in QUEST Program I this week to learn and practice social skills. The story we read to introduce our new skill was called:

Joining In

Together we have learned:

- Ways to join in a group on the playground.

- How to determine if it is a good time to try to join a group.

- Why it is important to observe groups before joining in.

You can help your child practice at home by:

- Inviting one or two of your child's friends over for a small group event. Limit time to less than one hour and plan activities.

- Helping your child observe group activities in their day-to-day experiences. Help your child determine if it would be a good idea to try to join each group. Discuss why it might be wise not to attempt to join some groups.

- Reminding them of the three steps used to join in a group when friends visit or when meeting groups of friends or family members:

    1. Stand at arm's length away;
    2. Smile;
    3. Say "Hi."

Thanks for your help!

QUEST Program I Social Skills Curriculum for Elementary School Students with Autism
© by JoEllen Cumpata and Susan Fell. Future Horizons, Inc.

Taking Turns - Story 3-3

Sometimes kids do things at the same time. When lots of kids are together, they might all talk at the same time. When kids play games, they might all play at the same time. When lots of kids are together, it's a good idea to take turns.

Taking turns helps kids learn. Taking turns helps kids be friends and have fun. Taking turns helps people feel calm and happy when they play or learn.

Sometimes adults decide how kids will take turns and who will go first. Kids can also decide to take turns without an adult helping.

When kids take turns, they need to go one at a time. When kids take turns talking, they need to talk and then listen to what the other kids say before talking again. When kids play a game, they need to take their turn and then let the other kids take their turns too. When kids play a game, it's okay to ask, "Is it my turn now?" or "Who goes next?"

Taking turns makes games and talking less confusing. Taking turns helps kids be happy and have friends. I can take turns by waiting and listening when I am playing or talking with others. I can ask if it is my turn if I'm not sure. I can wait until the person next to me has a turn and then take mine when they are done. Taking turns is a smart way to play and learn.

Taking Turns - Activity Sheet 3-3

Name _____

1. Find these words or phrases in the story and highlight them:

   time   turns   decide

   waiting   same   learn

2. Look at the pictures below. Tell a story about why it's important for the kids in the picture to take turns.

Taking Turns - Activity Sheet 3-3

Materials

- Taking Turns story
- Taking Turns - Matching Memory Game cards
- Taking Turns - Matching Memory Game Rules poster
- Taking Turns arrows
- Poster sticky tack

Procedure

- Prior to class, cut out "Taking Turns" Matching Memory Game - cards.
- Read "Taking Turns" story
- Show students an example of two matching cards from "Taking Turns" Matching Memory Game.
- Tell students you are going to play a fun game, and each student will have a chance to choose the rules.
- Read the "Taking Turns" Matching Memory Game Rules poster.
- Select one student to choose four rules from the poster.
- Place "Taking Turns" arrows on select rules using sticky tack.
- Each student will take turns placing a "Taking Turns" Matching Memory Game card upside down on the table.
- Play the game.
- Voice praise for those who demonstrate good turn-taking skills.
- If students select rules which promote confusion, arguments, or chaos, explain why turn-taking helps to avoid confusion and anger, and students will have more fun.

Taking Turns - Matching Memory Game Rules 3-3

Pick four rules from the list below. Put arrows next to the rules you choose.

The oldest goes first.

The youngest goes first.

Everyone plays at the same time.

One person plays at a time.

Play goes to the right.

Play goes to the left.

Take two match cards at a time.

Take as many matches as you want.

If you don't match, your turn ends.

If you match, take another turn.

QUEST Program I Social Skills Curriculum for Elementary School Students with Autism
© by JoEllen Cumpata and Susan Fell. Future Horizons, Inc.

Taking Turns - Matching Memory Game Arrows 3-3

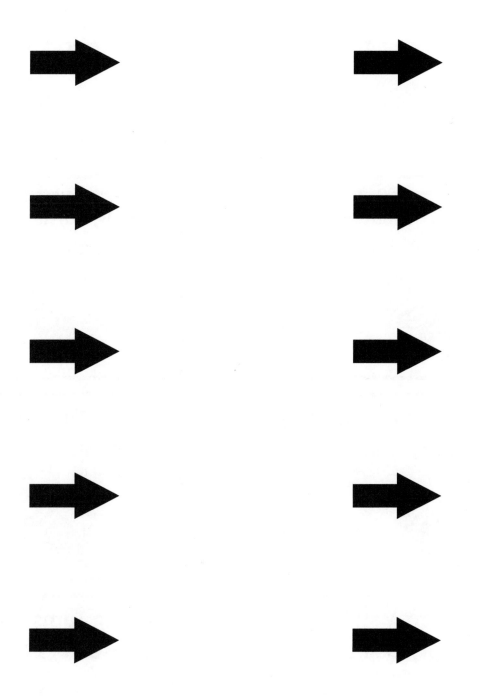

Taking Turns - Matching Memory Game Cards 3-3

Taking Turns Matching
Memory Game

Taking Turns Matching
Memory Game

Taking Turns Matching
Memory Game

Taking Turns Matching
Memory Game

Taking Turns Matching
Memory Game

Taking Turns Matching
Memory Game

Taking Turns Matching
Memory Game

QUEST Program I Social Skills Curriculum for Elementary School Students with Autism

Taking Turns - Matching Memory Game Cards 3-3

Taking Turns - Matching Memory Game Cards 3-3

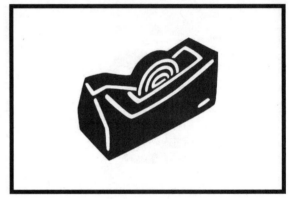

Taking Turns - Matching Memory Game Cards 3-3

Taking Turns - Matching Memory Game Cards 3-3

Taking Turns - Report 3-3

Names_____

Date_____

Directions: Read the sentences below. Fill in the blanks for each question. Look at the story or use the word box if you need help.

1. Sometimes kids talk or play at the same _____.

2. When lots of kids are together, it's a good idea to _____ turns.

3. Taking turns helps kids learn, be _____, and feel calm and happy when they play or learn.

4. Sometimes _____decide how kids will take turns and who will go first.

5. Kids can also decide to take _____ without an adult helping.

6. When kids take turns, they need to go _____ at a time.

7. When kids take turns talking, they need to talk and then _____ to what the other kids say before talking again.

8. When kids play a game, they need to take their turn, and then
    _____ until the others take their turn to go again.

9. When kids play a game, it's okay to _____ "Is it my turn
    now?" or "Who goes next?"

10. Taking turns makes games and talking fun and less
    _____.

WORD BOX

one	wait	time
confusing	listen	friends
adults	turns	ask
take		

QUEST Program I UPDATE!

Dear Parent,

Your child has been working hard in QUEST Program I this week to learn and practice social skills. The story we read to introduce our new skill was called:

Taking Turns

Together we have learned:

- The importance for taking turns in school. It helps students have fun, be respectful, and learn.

- The procedures to follow when taking turns.

- Ways to ask for clarification when taking turns if unsure of the process.

You can help your child practice at home by:

- Use taking turns regularly during household activities.

    e.g., "Johnny, you get to pick the first TV show and Billy, you can pick the second one. How does that sound?"

    "I know everyone has something fun to share about their day. Let's start with Dad and go around the table to take turns talking."

    "I know you are all excited to have your turn. Lynn, how should we decide who goes first?"

- Model asking for clarification when playing a game with your child.

    e.g., "Sam, I forgot who went last. When will it be my turn?"

Thanks for your help!

Pretending and Acting Silly - Story 3-4

Most kids like to laugh, goof around, and act silly. If kids laugh, goof around, and act silly in class they might get into trouble. It is important for kids to know when they can act silly, so teachers and other students don't get angry.

Teachers want kids to listen in class. Sometimes kids act silly by talking when the teacher is talking. Sometimes kids act silly by making noises. Sometimes kids act silly by throwing things or even getting out of their seats when they are not supposed to. Sometimes kids act silly by making faces or telling jokes. Teachers get angry when students act silly in class.

After school or at recess kids can act silly. Acting silly on the playground is another way to have fun. Kids might act silly by doing cartwheels, somersaults, making funny faces, making noises, or telling jokes. Running, throwing balls, playing games, yelling, jumping, acting silly, and pretending are all okay on the playground.

I can try to not act silly in class. I can act silly on the playground or after school. Teachers will not be angry when I wait until I'm on the playground to act silly. Waiting until I am on the playground to play, act silly, and pretend are good ways to have fun.

QUEST Program I Social Skills Curriculum for Elementary School Students with Autism
© by JoEllen Cumpata and Susan Fell. Future Horizons, Inc.

Pretending and Acting Silly - Activity Sheet 3-4

Name _____

1. Find these words or phrases in the story and highlight them:

   silly   playground   class

   teachers   angry   fun

2. The pictures below show students pretending and acting silly.
   Tell a story about one of the pictures below.

---

3. Circle the times it is okay to have fun, pretend, or act silly. Put an 'X' over the times it is not okay to have fun, pretend, or act silly.

in math class   at recess

during dinner   outside

in the lunchroom   during a fire drill

if you are in a play   in the swimming pool

Pretending and Acting Silly - Activity Sheet 3-4

Materials

- Pretending and Acting Silly story

- Pretending and Acting Silly handouts

- Pencils

Procedure

- Read "Pretending and Acting Silly" story.

- Divide students into groups of two or three.

- Pass a "Pretending and Acting Silly" handout to each group.

- Ask groups to discuss and complete the handout.

- Discuss responses as a group.

Pretending and Acting Silly - Handout 3-4

Directions: Look at the word box and at the statements. Choose the right answer from the word box and fill in the blanks.

1. Most kids like to _____ and act silly.

2. Teachers might get _____ if kids act silly at the wrong time, like in class.

3. Usually, teachers want students to sit still and be _____ in class.

4. _____ is a good time to act silly, play, and even pretend.

5. Pretending is a good way to use your _____.

6. Most kids like to pretend that they are animals, movie or sports stars, or even _____.

7. When students are silly, they usually like to _____.

8. Kids might act silly on the playground by doing summersaults, making funny _____, or telling jokes.

WORD BOX
pretend
laugh
faces
angry
imagination
monsters
quiet
Recess

Pretending and Acting Silly - Role-Play Activity Sheet 3-4

Materials

- Pretending and Acting Silly story

- Pretending and Acting Silly role-play cards

Procedure

- Prior to class, cut out "Pretending and Acting Silly" role-play cards.

- Read "Pretending and Acting Silly" story.

- Place "Pretending and Acting Silly" role-play cards face down on the table.

- Ask students to choose card and pretend to be the character on the card.

- Ask the group to guess who or what the student is pretending to be.

- Ask the group to discuss what movements, facial expressions, or words were used to act out the card.

- Allow the student who correctly guesses to go next.

Pretending and Acting Silly - Role-Play Cards 3-4

Pretend you are the principal.

Pretend you are a grandparent.

Pretend you are a doctor.

Pretend you are a teacher.

Pretend you are a mother.

Pretend you are a father.

Pretend you are a ballerina.

Pretend you are a scientist.

Pretending and Acting Silly - Role-Play Cards 3-4

Pretend you are a lion.

Pretend you are a monster.

Pretend you are a dinosaur.

Pretend you are a dog.

Pretend you are a robot.

Pretend you are a bird.

Pretend you are a fish.

Pretend you are a superhero.

Pretending and Acting Silly - Report 3-4

Names_____

Date_____

Directions: Read the sentences below. Fill in the blanks for each question. Look at the story or use the word box if you need help.

1. Most kids like to laugh, goof around, and act _____.

2. If kids laugh, goof around, and act silly in _____ they might get into trouble.

3. It is _____ for kids to know when they can act silly, so teachers and other students don't get angry.

4. _____ want kids to listen in class.

5. Sometimes kids act silly by making noises, _____ things, making faces, or telling jokes.

6. Teachers get _____ when students act silly in class.

7. After school or at _____ kids can act silly.

8. Acting silly on the playground is another way to have _____.

QUEST Program I Social Skills Curriculum for Elementary School Students with Autism
© by JoEllen Cumpata and Susan Fell. Future Horizons, Inc.

9. Running, throwing balls, playing _____, yelling, jumping, and acting silly are all okay on the playground.

WORD BOX

fun	important	games
Teachers	class	recess
silly	angry	throwing

QUEST Program I UPDATE!

Dear Parent,

Your child has been working hard in QUEST Program I this week to learn and practice social skills. The story we read to introduce our new skill was called:

Pretending and Acting Silly

Together we have learned:

- That most kids like to pretend and act silly sometimes.

- Why some times are better than others for acting silly and pretending.

- Where and how students pretend and act silly in appropriate ways.

You can help your child practice at home by:

- Reminding your child of appropriate times for silliness and pretending.

    e.g., "We are all so excited for our vacation, but, Andrew, I really need you to get dressed now. There will be time for silly play at the lake."

- Helping your child recognize pretending and silly play opportunities.

    e.g., "Look at Josh and Brian. What kind of animals do they look like? I bet you could make a noise like a pig too!"

Thanks for your help!

Winning, Losing, and Being a Good Sport - Story 3-5

Friends like to play games together. Kids play sit down games like card games, video games, or board games. Kids play standing and running games like tag or football. Games have rules. Games have winners and losers. Games are fun, but most kids like it best when they are the winner.

Playing games is usually not fun when someone gets angry, cries, or fights. Kids might not want to play with someone again if they are always getting angry, crying, or fighting when they lose a game. This is called being a poor sport, or a sore loser.

Kids like to play with other kids who are happy, even if they lose a game. This is called being a good sport. Good sports usually:

- Know the rules of the game;

- Try to act happy even if they don't win;

- Congratulate the winner by saying, "Great game!"

I can be a good sport when I play games. I can act happy even when I lose, and I can congratulate the winner. When I'm a good sport, I can have fun even if I lose, and friends will ask me to play with them again.

Winning, Losing, and Being a Good Sport - Activity Sheet 3-5

```
I  P  U  T  R  L  H  F  R  I  E  N  D  S  K  J
T  G  J  K  L  O  F  R  T  Y  U  I  O  M  N  B
Z  X  C  V  B  S  N  M  E  F  A  S  D  P  F  G
X  C  F  G  B  E  S  D  F  U  N  U  P  L  R  T
L  K  J  H  G  F  D  S  A  Q  W  E  R  A  M  S
C  V  B  N  J  E  R  T  Y  U  I  C  M  Y  M  C
P  O  I  U  Y  T  R  E  W  Q  A  H  X  C  V  H
A  S  D  F  G  H  J  K  L  T  V  E  H  G  T  O
W  I  N  N  E  R  G  F  R  O  I  E  L  K  J  O
Z  X  C  V  B  G  F  O  R  E  W  R  P  O  I  L
V  B  N  H  P  O  P  Y  T  R  E  W  Q  A  S  D
X  C  V  B  U  S  P  O  I  U  R  U  L  E  S  M
M  N  B  V  D  V  C  X  Z  A  S  D  F  G  H  J
Q  W  E  O  Y  U  I  A  N  G  R  Y  P  O  I  U
B  V  O  K  U  H  T  F  R  D  E  C  F  G  C  L
L  G  G  H  C  O  N  G  R  A  T  U  L  A  T  E
```

QUEST Program I Social Skills Curriculum for Elementary School Students with Autism
© by JoEllen Cumpata and Susan Fell. Future Horizons, Inc.

Find and circle these words and phrases

Friends	Good Sport	Rules
Fun	Congratulate	Winner
Lose	Play	Angry

Answer Key

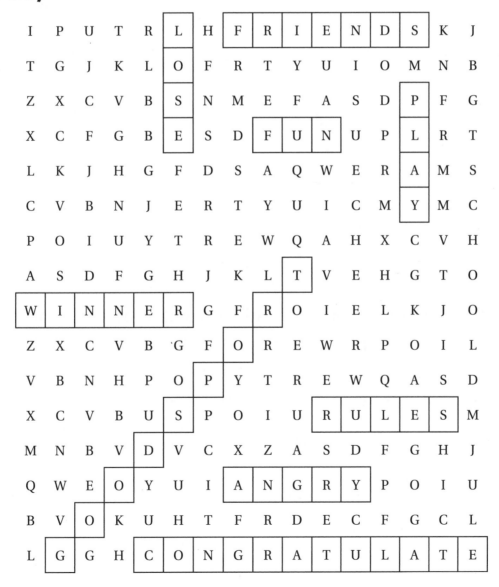

Winning, Losing, and Being a Good Sport - Report 3-5

Names_____

Date_____

Directions: Read the sentences below. Fill in the blanks for each question. Look at the story or use the word box if you need help.

1. Friends like to play games _____.

2. Games have _____.

3. _____ have winners and losers.

4. Games are fun, but most kids like it best when they are the _____.

5. Playing games is usually not fun when someone gets _____, cries, or fights.

6. Kids might not want to play with someone again if they are a "_____ _____," or a "sore loser."

7. Kids like to play with other kids who are happy. This is called being a _____ _____.

8. Good sports usually:

- _____ the rules of the game;

- Try to act _____ even if they don't win;

- _____ the winner by saying, "Great game!"

WORD BOX

rules	Congratulate	angry
poor sport	Know	together
winner	good sport	happy
Games		

QUEST Program I UPDATE!

Dear Parent,

Your child has been working hard in QUEST Program I this week to learn and practice social skills. The story we read to introduce our new skill was called:

Winning, Losing, and Being a Good Sport

Together we have learned:

- That most kids enjoy winning.

- Games can be fun and interesting, even when we don't win.

- Ways to be a good sport include:
  1. Knowing the rules of the game;
  2. Trying to be happy even when losing;
  3. Congratulating the winner by saying, "Great game!"

You can help your child practice at home by:

- Modeling good sportsmanship yourself.

  e.g., "Oh my, I really wanted to win that tennis match with Mrs. Jones. I just wanted to throw my racket when I lost, but I didn't. Did you see me shake her hand? That was really hard for me to do!"

- Helping your child to negotiate rules before beginning a game with others.

- Complimenting your child when they handle disappointment well.

  e.g., "I noticed you told Stephen, "Good game!" after he won. That was a very grown up way to be a good sport."

Thanks for your help!

Sharing Friends - Story 3-6

Some kids have one friend and some have two or more. It is okay to have one friend. It's okay to have lots of friends. Friends make our day at school fun and interesting.

Sometimes kids get worried that people will not like them or that their friends will decide they want to spend time with someone else. Some kids get angry if anyone talks or spends time with their friend because they are worried they will lose that friend.

Everyone has choices, and we all get to choose our friends. Friends can decide who they want to talk to, who they want to spend time with during the day and at lunch. All students have choices, but we can't choose for someone else.

It is okay for students to stay friends for a long time, and it is okay to change friends. If students see their friend spending time with someone else, they can try to join in by:

- Standing at arm's length away.
- Smiling.
- Saying "Hi."
- Joining in the conversation.

If the other kids don't want to be friends anymore, say "Go away" or use other mean words, it's a good time to find new friends.

Friends don't spend time together every day. It is okay to hang out one day and not the next, and still be friends. It's okay to spend time with different people or just each other.

I can have friends, and my friends and I can have choices. I can spend time with friends or decide not to. If my friends don't want to hang out one day, I can try to spend time with them later or go find someone else. It's nice to have choices, and it's nice to have friends.

Sharing Friends - Activity Sheet 3-6

Name _____

1. Find these words or phrases in the story and highlight them:

   choices   angry   friends

   someone   different   decide

2. Circle the things we should do when we have friends. Put an 'X' over the things we should NOT do when we have friends.

   Tell our friend, "They can't hang out with anyone else."

   Eat lunch and play together.

   Get angry if our friend has lunch with someone else.

   Choose our own friends.

   Let our friends choose other friends too.

   Let other kids join in.

Sharing Friends - Activity Sheet 3-6

Materials

- Sharing Friends story
- Sharing Friends cut and paste activity sheet
- Magazines
- Scissors
- Glue
- Crayons

Alternate Activity: Students can draw pictures, or actual photographs of students can be used. Photographs for the project can be taken with a digital camera, printed, and used in the activity.

Procedure

- Read "Sharing Friends" story.
- Hand out "Sharing Friends" cut and paste activity sheet and supplies.
- Ask students to think about their friends or students they would like as friends.
- Allow students to look through magazines and find pictures of children playing alone and with one, two, and more friends.
- Tell students they are to cut out pictures, and paste in appropriate spaces on the "Sharing Friends" cut and paste activity sheet.
- Ask students to write their first name and the names of their friends on the activity sheet.
- Ask students to write activities they like to do alone and with others.
- Have students share their completed project with the group.

Sharing Friends - Activity 3-6

I like to share friends.

These are things I like to do with friends.

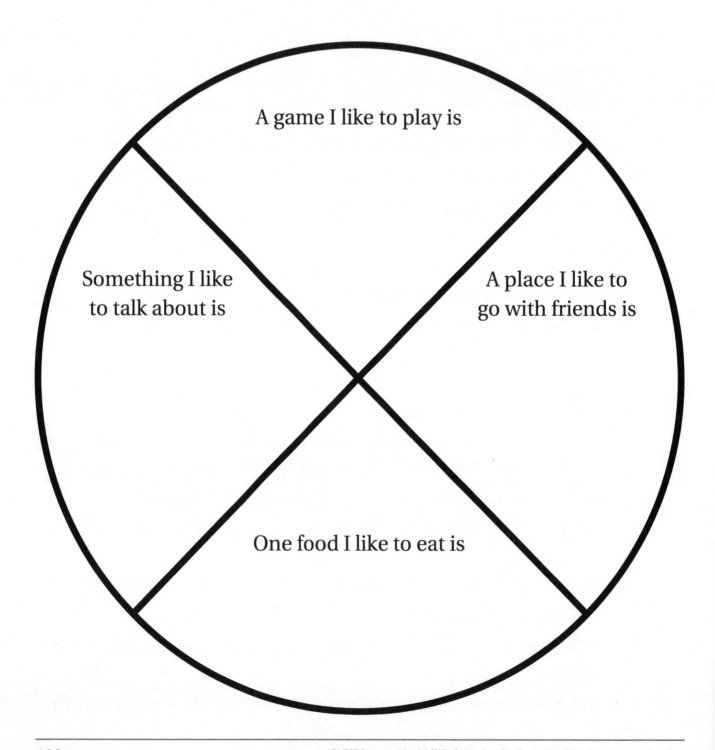

1. Some of my friends' names:

_____   _____

_____   _____

2. Plan a fun day with one of the friends above (use the ideas from your circle on the other side).

I will spend time with: _____

This is what we will do together:

_____

_____

_____

3. Tell the class a story about the day you have planned.

Sharing Friends - Report 3-6

Names_____

Date_____

Directions: Read the sentences below. Fill in the blanks for each question. Look at the story or use the word box if you need help.

1. It is okay to have one friend, and it's okay to have lots of _____.

2. Friends make our day at school fun and _____.

3. Some kids get angry if anyone talks or spends time with their friend because they are _____ they will lose that friend.

4. Everyone has choices, and we all get to _____ our friends.

5. All students have choices, but we can't _____ for someone else.

6. It is okay for students to stay friends for a long time, and it is okay to _____ friends.

7. If students see their friend spending time with someone else they can try to _____ in by standing at arm's length away, smiling, and saying "Hi."

8. If the other kids don't want to be friends anymore and say "Go away", or if they use other _____ _____, it's a good time to find new friends.

9. It's okay to spend time with _____ people or just each other.

```
┌─────────────────────────────────────────────────────────────┐
│                       WORD BOX                                │
│                                                               │
│     change            different            interesting        │
│                                                               │
│     worried          mean words               join            │
│                                                               │
│     decide            choose                 friends           │
│                                                               │
└─────────────────────────────────────────────────────────────┘
```

QUEST Program I UPDATE!

Dear Parent,

Your child has been working hard in QUEST Program I this week to learn and practice social skills. The story we read to introduce our new skill was called:

Sharing Friends

Together we have learned:

- Some children have one friend, while others have more than one friend.
- All children may choose their own friends, but they may not choose for someone else.
- Children can join a group of friends by:
  1. Standing at arm's length away.
  2. Smiling.
  3. Saying "Hi."
  4. Asking, "Can I play with you?"

You can help your child practice at home by:

- Recognizing that your child may be sensitive, insecure, or even angry when their friends play with others.

- Encouraging play with multiple friends.

  e.g., "I know you are disappointed that Sally is playing with Jill today. Maybe she will want to play tomorrow. Who else can you call today?"
  "Jason is a very fun boy, and I'm not surprised he has lots of friends. It's okay that he's busy today. You have lots of friends too. Let me know when you decide what you want to do today."

Thanks for your help!

Calling Friends on the Telephone - Story 3-7

Kids like to hang out together during school. Kids also like to hang out together outside of school. When kids want to hang out, they need to make plans ahead of time. Sometimes kids make plans using the telephone.

Before you call a friend to hang out:

- Talk with your parents about what you want to do.
- Find your friend's telephone number.
- Dial the number, introduce yourself, and ask to speak with your friend.
- Talk about what you want to do.
- Have a pencil and paper ready to write down plans.
- Say "Good-bye" when you are all done planning.

Kids need to decide what to do together. Kids need to decide when they are getting together. Kids need to decide where they will get together. Kids need to decide how they will get where they are going.

Parents need to help with a plan. Parents can help plan a snack. Parents can help plan who will drive. Parents can help plan what kids can do together.

Getting together with kids is fun, but kids need to plan! Kids can plan by talking with their friend. Kids can plan by talking with their parent. When kids use the telephone, they can plan for a fun day.

Calling Friends on the Telephone - Activity Sheet 3-7

Name _____

1. Find these words or phrases in the story and highlight them:

   number   parents   decide

   ready   hang out   plans

2. Look at your "Calling Friends on the Telephone" - Activity Sheet. Fill out the "Telephone Planning Card" below to get ready to call your friend and hang out.

Telephone Planning Card

The person I'm calling is _____

Their telephone number is _____

This is my plan for hanging out:

    The place _____

    The day _____

    The time _____

What we will do together _____

Who will drive _____

Calling Friends on the Telephone - Activity Sheet 3-7

Materials

- Calling Friends on the Telephone story

- Telephone Planning Card

- Landline or cell phones

- My Telephone Log handout for each student.

Procedure

- Read "Calling Friends on the Telephone" story.

- Use phones to practice calling the person on each student's Telephone Planning Card.

- Create more Telephone Planning Cards if students want to try calling other students.

- Hand out My Telephone Log.

- Let students know for homework, they will need to call the student on their Telephone Planning Card and document it on their My Telephone Log.

- Students who complete their log can earn an incentive.

My Telephone Log

Date	Who I called	What we planned	Did our plans happen?	
			YES	NO

Calling Friends on the Telephone - Report 3-7

Names_____

Date_____

Directions: Read the sentences below. Fill in the blanks for each question. Look at the story or use the word box if you need help.

1. Kids like to _____ _____together during school.

2. Kids also like to hang out together _____ of school.

3. When kids want to hang out, they need to make _____ ahead of time.

4. Sometimes kids make plans using the _____.

5. Before you call a friend to hang out you should:

   a. Talk with your _____ about what you want to do.

   b. Find your friend's telephone number.

   c. Dial the _____ and ask to speak with your friend.

   d. Talk about what you want to do.

   e. Have a _____ and paper ready to write down plans.

f. Say_____-_____ when you are all done planning.

6. Parents need to help plan a snack, who will drive, and what kids can do _____.

WORD BOX

pencil	parents	outside
plans	telephone	together
good-bye	hang out	number

QUEST Program I UPDATE!

Dear Parent,

Your child has been working hard in QUEST Program I this week to learn and practice social skills. The story we read to introduce our new skill was called:

Calling Friends on the Telephone

Together we have learned:

- Why the telephone is important when making plans with friends.
- How to share information with friends on the telephone.

You can help your child practice at home by:

- Helping your child decide who they can call on the telephone and what information they will share

  e.g., "Why don't you give Katie a call to make sure she is coming with us to the mall tomorrow?"
- Using the Telephone Planning Card below to help your child rehearse telephone conversations before calls.

Telephone Planning Card

The person I'm calling is _____

Their telephone number is _____

This is my plan for hanging out:

    The place _____

    The day _____

    The time _____

What we will do together _____

Who will drive _____

Thanks for your help!

Dealing with Mean Kids - Story 3-8

Everybody gets to pick their friends. Friends can hang out together one day and not the next. It is okay to have different friends and not spend time together all the time. Kids also have fun in different ways.

When they have fun, some kids act silly, joke, push, and tease in a fun way. Kids can get rough, run, push, and yell when they are outside. Some kids don't like the rough-play, while some do. If kids don't like to rough-play, they can ask the others to stop, or they can walk away and find another group of students to hang out with.

Once in a while, a student will try to be mean or rough on purpose. They will not stop even after being asked. Sometimes a student will say mean words, push, or hurt another kid on purpose. This can happen even after they have been asked to stop or the kid tries to walk away.

If a kid doesn't stop saying mean words, pushing, or teasing, even after being asked; it is time to get an adult to help. It is never okay for a student to tell another student they will hurt them. It is important for all students to be safe at school. Adults are there to help when kids get too rough or mean.

I can run, play, and yell outside if I want to. I can decide who I want to hang around with. I can ask rough students to stop or I can spend time with students who are calm and quiet. If students don't stop when I ask, I can get an adult to help. Kids need to be safe when they are together.

Dealing with Mean Kids - Activity Sheet 3-8

Name _____

1. Find these words or phrases in the story and highlight them:

   okay   rough   together

   tease   quiet   adults

2. Circle the things we should do when we are dealing with mean
   kids. Put an 'X' over the things we should NOT do when we are
   dealing with mean kids.

   walk away   punch them

   cry   ask them to stop

   tell an adult   hang out with nice kids

   call them names   tell other kids

Dealing with Mean Kids - Activity Sheet 3-8

Materials

- Dealing with Mean Kids story

- Dealing with Mean Kids scenario cards

- Mean/Not Mean game board

- Thumbs Up/Thumbs Down cards

Procedure

- Prior to class, cut out "Dealing with Mean Kids - scenario cards. Hold scenario cards and ask students to choose one.
- Read "Dealing with Mean Kids" story.
- Ask the student to read the card aloud.
- Ask the student to decide if they think the student described on the card was being mean or not mean. Have them put the card in the appropriate place on the "Mean/Not Mean" game board.
- Ask the student to tell the group how he/she would handle the situation on the card.
- Ask the group to use their "Thumbs Up/Thumbs Down" cards to indicate if they feel the student's response was appropriate.
- Discuss.

Dealing with Mean Kids - Scenario Cards 3-8

One of your friends says, "They want to have lunch with someone else."

You see one of your friends hanging out with someone else on the playground.

A boy from your class pushes you when you are outside and says, "Watch where you're going, dummy!"

You see a boy from your class hitting another boy. Both boys are laughing.

All the swings are taken. You ask the students to get off, so you can have a turn, but they don't.

You usually walk home with one of your neighbors. He tells you he can't walk with you today.

You walk up to a group of kids playing basketball and ask them if you can play? They say "No."

After school a girl is running past and bumps into you. She says "Sorry!"

Dealing with Mean Kids - Scenario Cards 3-8

A group of kids are playing a rough game at lunch. You want to play, but you don't like rough games.

The kids you usually eat lunch with didn't save you a seat.

A group of kids are laughing and keep calling each other "stupid head."

Your best friend says, "She can't come over after school because she's going to another friend's house."

A boy you don't know very well is having a birthday party and he doesn't invite you.

A girl in your class brings cupcakes to school for everyone, but she won't let you have one.

A boy in PE class kicks you and takes the ball you were playing with.

You see an older boy walking home from school. He runs by you and says, "Out of my way, kid!"

Dealing with Mean Kids - Scenario Cards 3-8

A student in your class accidentally dumps water on your project. He tries to clean it up, but makes a bigger mess.

A student in your class tells another student she doesn't like you.

Your best friend says, "He's mad at you."

Your best friend says, "You can't come over anymore because you broke his video controller."

You are playing a board game with two kids and another kid walks up and says, "That game is for babies!"

You are using the computer and another student says, "Hurry up, slowpoke! I need to get on!"

Your friends want to play a computer game that you think is boring.

Your friends like to play football and roll on the lawn. You don't like to roll on the lawn.

Dealing with Mean Kids - Game Board 3-8

The student on the card was acting MEAN

The student on the card was NOT acting MEAN

QUEST Program I Social Skills Curriculum for Elementary School Students with Autism
© by JoEllen Cumpata and Susan Fell. Future Horizons, Inc.

Thumbs Up/Thumbs Down - Cards 3-8

Dealing with Mean Kids - Report 3-8

Names_____

Date_____

Directions: Read the sentences below. Fill in the blanks for each question. Look at the story or use the word box if you need help.

1. Everybody gets to pick their _____.

2. It is okay to have different friends and not spend time _____ all the time.

3. Some kids like to joke, push, run, tease in a fun way, and yell when they are _____.

4. Some kids _____ like to play rough, while some do.

5. If kids don't like rough-play, they can _____ the others to stop or walk away.

6. Once in a while, a student will try to be mean or rough ____ _____ and won't stop.

7. If a student doesn't stop saying mean words, pushing, or teasing even after being asked; it is time to get an _____ to help.

8. It is _____ okay for a student to tell another student they will hurt them.

9. It is important for all students to be _____.

WORD BOX

safe	on purpose	ask
together	never	friends
outside	don't	adult

QUEST Program I UPDATE!

Dear Parent,

Your child has been working hard in QUEST Program I this week to learn and practice social skills. The story we read to introduce our new skill was called:

Dealing with Mean Kids

Together we have learned:

- That it is not unusual for children to yell, push, call names, and play rough during play times.

- That not all children like rough-play.

- That all children have a choice when it comes to choosing friends, and the play style they are most comfortable with.

- Ways to leave an uncomfortable play situation and get adult assistance if needed.

You can help your child practice at home by:

- Listening to your child's interpretation of their school day and helping them discover and appreciate different styles of play.

  e.g., "Boy, it sounds like Mike really likes to play rough."

  "I know you've told me before how Erin likes to be quiet when she plays."

  "I've watched your friends play after school, and I see them running and screaming a lot. I think you were smart to get your teacher. It sounds like that play situation got too rough."

- Helping your child determine their own tolerance and response to rough-play.

  e.g., "When Sandy pushed you today, what did you do?"

  "I guess if you are not comfortable with the pushing in a football game, you have two choices. You can play and be a bit uncomfortable, or watch and be comfortable."

  "Seems to me you prefer to play quietly with Sam. Why don't you call him today?"

- Observe your child at play and help them negotiate play rules when necessary.

Thanks for your help!

QUEST Program I Parent/Teacher Evaluation Unit 3 - Having Friends

Student Name _____ Date _____

Parent/Teacher Name _____

The past several weeks in QUEST Program I we have been focusing on Getting Along with Friends.

Please complete the rating scale below to assist us in determining how well the student has generalized the skills taught. Check the boxes which identify how often you have observed the skills listed during the past few weeks.

Skill	Does Independently	Does Only With Adult Reminders	Improvement Noted (Post-test only)
Making Friends at School: Approaching peers, standing an arm's length away, smiling and saying, "Hi."			
Joining In: Recognizing appropriate times to approach peer groups, making an attempt to approach group, using greetings appropriately.			
Taking Turns: Clarifying rules before beginning a game, demonstrating an understanding of the need for turn-taking, showing patience.			
Acting Silly: Acting silly at appropriate times, refraining from silly play at school and quiet moments at home, tolerating pretend play in others, attempting pretend play with peers.			
Winning, Losing and Being A Good Sport: Clarifying rules before beginning a game, showing stamina when not successful in a game/sport, tolerating loss, congratulating a winner.			
Sharing Friends: Demonstrating desire for friendships, demonstrating comfort level around multiple peers, allowing peers to interact with others.			
Calling Friends on the Telephone: Using appropriate skills/strategies when talking on the telephone to make a social arrangement with a friend.			

Skill	Does Independently	Does Only With Adult Reminders	Improvement Noted (Post-test only)
Dealing with Mean Kids: Appreciating and recognizing different play styles in peers, refraining from resorting to tattletale when others are playing rough, choosing peers who have similar tolerance for rough play, appropriately seeking adult assistance when physically or verbally threatened or hurt.			

Comments_____

_____

Thank you for your input!

© by JoEllen Cumpata and Susan Fell. Future Horizons, Inc.

Unit 4

Everybody Has Feelings

Goal and Objectives Unit 4 - Everybody Has Feelings

Goal

To learn about emotions and emotional responses in yourself and others.

Objectives

➤ To understand that all people experience emotions.

➤ To recognize emotions in yourself and express how you are feeling to others.

➤ To use and recognize the meaning of body language in self and others.

➤ To learn appropriate ways to manage anger.

➤ To develop an understanding of empathy and ways to comfort those in need.

Stories, Activities, and Parent Updates

Stories can be read by parents, teachers, or students. Often students gain a deeper understanding of skills when stories are discussed in detail in a group setting. Asking students to summarize paragraphs, relate their personal experiences, and complete activities are all effective ways to increase generalization of skills. Parent Updates provide additional ways to continue learning at home.

Topics included in this unit are:

1. I Have Feelings

2. Telling People How I Feel

3. Faces and Bodies Can Talk

4. Everybody Gets Angry Sometimes

5. Comforting Others

I Have Feelings - Story 4-1

Everybody has feelings. Some feelings are good like being happy or being excited. Some feelings are bad like being angry, scared, or sad.

It's easy to tell when babies have feelings. Babies cry, kick, laugh, or move their bodies. When older kids and grown-ups have feelings, sometimes it is not as easy to tell. You need to watch closely. If you watch closely, you can see on their faces how people are feeling. If you watch closely, you might be able to tell how people feel by how they move their hands, feet, and bodies.

Showing people how we feel in our face and body is a good idea when we are happy. When we are happy, we can smile or laugh.

But older kids and grown-ups should not always show bad feelings. Grown-ups and older kids should not kick or throw like babies when they are upset.

When we are feeling bad, it's smart to talk about it. Telling people how we are feeling will help them know how to help.

I can watch for feelings on people's faces and bodies. I can show people how I am feeling too. If I'm upset, I can talk about it.

QUEST Program I Social Skills Curriculum for Elementary School Students with Autism

I Have Feelings - Activity Sheet 4-1

Name _____

1. Find these words or phrases in the story and highlight them:

   laugh   babies   talk

   upset   happy   face

2. Tell a story about one of the pictures below. How are they feeling? How do you know? What would you say or do if you saw this person?

I Have Feelings - Report 4-1

Names_____

Date_____

Directions: Read the sentences below. Fill in the blanks for each question. Look at the story or use the word box if you need help.

1. Everybody has _____.

2. Some feelings are good, like being _____ or being excited.

3. Some feelings are bad, like being _____, scared or sad.

4. It's easy to tell when babies have feelings, because they cry, kick, laugh, or move their _____.

5. When older kids and grown-ups have feelings, sometimes it is not as easy to tell, so you need to _____ closely.

6. If you watch closely, you can see how people are feeling on their _____and by how they move their hands, feet, and bodies.

7. When we are happy, we can smile or _____.

QUEST Program I Social Skills Curriculum for Elementary School Students with Autism
© by JoEllen Cumpata and Susan Fell. Future Horizons, Inc.

8. But older kids and grown-ups should not kick or throw like _____ when they are upset.

9. When we are feeling bad, it's smart to _____ about it.

10. Telling _____ how we are feeling will help them know how to help.

WORD BOX

watch	people	laugh
talk	happy	bodies
feelings	babies	faces
angry		

QUEST Program I UPDATE!

Dear Parent,

Your child has been working hard in QUEST Program I this week to learn and practice social skills. The story we read to introduce our new skill was called:

I Have Feelings

Together we have learned:

- That all people have feelings.

- Ways to look for and show feelings on our faces and through body language.

- The best way to let others know we have angry or sad feelings is by talking about them.

You can help your child practice at home by:

- Talking with a "feelings" vocabulary.

    e.g., "I know you can see on my face that I'm angry right now, so it might not be a good time to ask for more."
    "I knew Grandma was happy because she smiled and gave us all a big hug."

- Encouraging discussion when your child is experiencing negative emotions.

    e.g., "It really helps me to talk about it when I'm upset. How about if we have a little chat after you relax in your room for a bit?"

Thanks for your help!

Telling People How I Feel - Story 4-2

Sometimes we feel happy. Sometimes we feel sad. Sometimes we feel angry. Sometimes we feel excited. Everybody has feelings. All feelings are okay.

When babies are upset, they kick, cry, throw things, yell, or make a fuss. It's okay for babies to do this because they can't tell us how they feel yet.

It's not okay for older kids or grown-ups to kick, cry, throw things, yell, or make a fuss. Kicking and throwing things can be dangerous. Yelling can make everyone even angrier.

We can use words to tell people how we feel. Older kids and grown-ups should use their words to tell other people how they feel. Using words to tell people how we feel is smart.

When we use our words, other people know how we feel. When we tell people how we feel, they know what to do.

Telling People How I Feel - Activity Sheet 4-2

Name _____

1. Find these words or phrases in the story and highlight them:

   feel   dangerous   smart

   sad   words   people

2. Draw a line to match the feeling below with the story. One is already done for you.

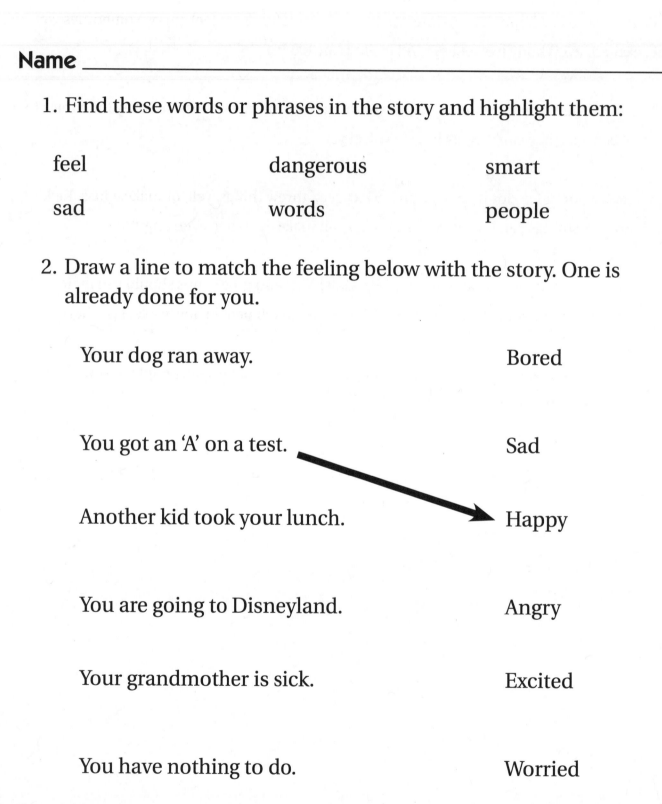

   Your dog ran away.   Bored

   You got an 'A' on a test.   Sad

   Another kid took your lunch.   Happy

   You are going to Disneyland.   Angry

   Your grandmother is sick.   Excited

   You have nothing to do.   Worried

QUEST Program I Social Skills Curriculum for Elementary School Students with Autism

Telling People How I Feel - Activity Sheet 4-2

Materials –

- Telling People How I Feel story
- Feelings Picture cards

Procedure –

- Prior to class, cut out "Feelings Picture" cards.

- Read "Telling People How I Feel" story aloud in class and discuss.

- Place "Feelings Picture" cards upside down on the table and allow students to choose one at a time.

- Ask the student to describe how they think the person is feeling.

- Discuss their response.

Feelings Picture - Cards 4-2

Feelings Picture - Cards 4-2

Telling People How I Feel - Report 4-2

Names_____

Date_____

Directions: Read the sentences below. Fill in the blanks for each question. Look at the story or use the word box if you need help.

1. We all feel happy, sad, angry, or excited because _____ has feelings.

2. All _____ are okay.

3. It's okay for babies to kick, cry, throw things, yell, or make a fuss, because they can't tell us how they _____ yet.

4. It's not _____ for older kids or grown-ups to kick, cry, throw things, yell, or make a fuss.

5. Kicking and throwing things can be _____.

6. Yelling can make everyone even _____.

7. We can use _____ to tell people how we feel.

8. When we use our words, other _____ know how we feel and what to do.

WORD BOX

words	dangerous	people
okay	feelings	everybody
angrier	feel	

QUEST Program I UPDATE!

Dear Parent,

Your child has been working hard in QUEST Program I this week to learn and practice social skills. The story we read to introduce our new skill was called:

Telling People How I Feel

Together we have learned:

- All feelings are okay.
- Talking about how we feel provides information to others.
- Becoming aggressive when we are upset is not okay.

You can help your child practice at home by:

- Modeling ways to express feelings.

  e.g., "Wow, I've had a really busy day. I feel so exhausted!"
  "I'm so excited about our trip!"

- Responding when your child expresses emotion.

  e.g., "Since you told me that you feel angry, I will let you stay in your room for a while, and then we can talk about it."
  "I'm glad you told me you feel worried about school tomorrow. Let's talk about what we can do to make it better for you."

Thanks for your help!

Faces and Bodies Can Talk - Story 4-3

Talking is a good way to let people know how we feel. When kids feel bad, talking about how they are feeling can help them feel better. When kids feel bad, talking about it may give other people information to help solve the problem.

We can tell people how we feel, but bodies and faces can tell about our feelings too.

When kids are happy, their eyes are usually wide open, their mouths are smiling, and their bodies are sitting or standing straight. Happy kids might even laugh.

When kids are angry, their bodies usually look different. Angry kids might stomp their feet, hit, cry, or even put their head down on their table or desk. When you look at the face of an angry person, you will see their eyebrows scrunch up and their mouth will frown.

Faces and bodies can tell us how someone is feeling. I can watch faces and bodies to see how my teacher, parents, and friends are feeling. I can show people how I am feeling with my face and body too.

Faces and Bodies Can Talk - Activity Sheet 4-3

Name _____

1. Find these words or phrases in the story and highlight them:

talking	solve	bodies
faces	feeling	look

2. Draw a picture of how the feelings might look on the faces below.

Sad

Worried

Confused

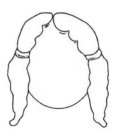

Angry

Excited

Happy

Faces and Bodies Can Talk - Report 4-3

Names_____

Date_____

Directions: Read the sentences below. Fill in the blanks for each question. Look at the story or use the word box if you need help.

1. Talking is a good way to let people know how we _____.

2. When kids feel bad, _____ about how they are feeling can help them feel better.

3. When kids feel bad, talking about it may even give other people _____ to help solve the problem.

4. We can tell people how we feel, but _____ and faces can tell us about feelings too.

5. When kids are _____, their eyes are usually wide open, their mouths are smiling, and their bodies are sitting or standing straight.

6. Happy kids might even _____.

7. When kids are _____, they might stomp their feet, hit, cry, or even put their head down on their table or desk.

8. When you look at the _____ of an angry person, you will see their eyebrows scrunch up, and their mouth will frown.

9. _____ faces and bodies can tell us how someone is feeling.

WORD BOX

face	angry	happy
Watching	talking	information
feel	laugh	bodies

QUEST Program I UPDATE!

Dear Parent,

Your child has been working hard in QUEST Program I this week to learn and practice social skills. The story we read to introduce our new skill was called:

Faces and Bodies Can Talk

Together we have learned:

- That people express feelings with words.
- That people can also show how they feel with facial expressions, gestures, and voice tone (body language).
- Watching for body language gives us more information about how people feel.

You can help your child practice at home by:

- Using and talking about body language

  e.g., "When your coach stomped his foot, I knew he was really angry!"

  "When you see me with my head down on the table, it means I'm tired and need you to be quiet. Can you talk to me later about this?"

Thanks for your help!

Everybody Gets Angry Sometimes - Story 4-4

Everybody has feelings. Everybody feels happy, sad, excited, bored, and even angry. Some people get angry every day; other people don't get angry that often. But everybody gets angry sometimes.

Some kids get angry when they don't win a game. Some kids get angry when they have to sit still and be quiet. Some kids get angry when their teacher asks them to do something they don't want to do.

Getting angry doesn't feel good. Getting angry can make our head or stomach hurt. Getting angry can make us feel hot. Getting angry might even make us do things that hurt ourselves or other people.

When kids get angry they might cry, put their head down, run away, yell, or even throw things. These are not good choices. Kids who yell or throw things are breaking school rules. Kids who cry, run and hide, or put their head down will not be able to work out their problem. When kids are angry, it is best to:

- Take a deep breath.
- Raise your hand.
- Talk with the teacher and try to work out the problem.

Teachers and parents want to be helpful, especially when students are angry. Talking with an adult is a smart way to feel better when we're angry.

I can try to tell an adult when I'm angry. I can take a deep breath, raise my hand, and talk with my teacher about my angry feelings. This is a good way to feel better in school.

Everybody Gets Angry Sometimes - Activity Sheet 4-4

Name _____

1. Find these words or phrases in the story and highlight them:

   everybody   angry   choices

   talk   breath   better

2. Look at the pictures below. Tell a story about why the person is angry and what they did about it.

3. Complete the word search below.

```
D  L  L  W  C  H  A  G  L  P  M  G  V  H  R  K
D  A  A  S  H  C  J  K  I  L  D  M  D  E  E  C
Q  H  N  U  P  L  O  P  S  P  B  E  G  L  H  P
D  G  J  G  M  K  K  K  T  S  V  H  A  P  J  K
G  F  K  Y  R  J  J  J  E  U  H  A  K  G  F  Q
O  D  Q  G  N  Y  H  H  N  T  E  A  C  H  E  R
P  S  W  T  B  D  G  G  I  D  Z  P  F  Y  H  S
R  A  E  R  V  G  F  F  N  D  X  C  A  H  R  M
O  M  N  B  V  C  X  D  G  F  G  V  H  E  G  N
B  Y  U  I  O  Z  Z  X  C  Y  U  B  R  N  R  E
L  D  E  E  P  Q  B  R  E  A  T  H  I  K  C  X
E  H  G  F  D  S  A  Z  X  C  P  K  B  N  M  L
M  K  I  U  Y  T  R  E  W  O  L  A  S  D  F  G
S  Q  W  E  R  T  Y  U  I  A  O  P  L  K  J  H
B  Y  U  P  O  I  U  H  T  R  E  D  S  A  Z  X
V  T  A  M  F  E  E  L  I  N  G  S  N  B  V  C
```

Find and circle these words and phrases

Listening	Deep breath	Talking	Problems
Help	Angry	Teacher	Feelings

Answer Key

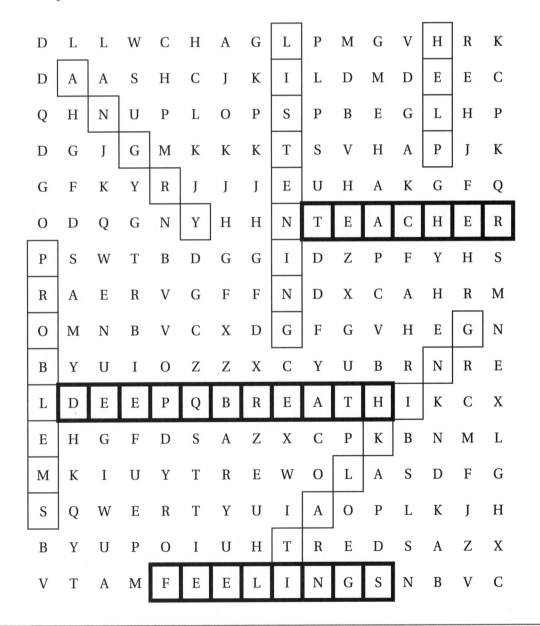

Everybody Gets Angry Sometimes - Report 4-4

Names_____

Date_____

Directions: Read the sentences below. Fill in the blanks for each question. Look at the story or use the word box if you need help.

1. Everybody feels happy, sad, excited, bored, and even
   _____.

2. Some people get angry every day, other people don't, but
   _____ gets angry sometimes.

3. Some kids get angry when they don't win a game, when they have to sit still, and be quiet or when their _____ asks them to do something they don't want to.

4. Getting angry doesn't _____good.

5. Getting angry can make our head or _____ hurt or make us feel hot.

6. Getting angry might even make us do things that _____ ourselves or other people.

7. Crying, yelling, or throwing things when we are angry is not a good _____.

QUEST Program I Social Skills Curriculum for Elementary School Students with Autism
© by JoEllen Cumpata and Susan Fell. Future Horizons, Inc.

8. Kids who yell or throw things are breaking school
_____ and will not be able to work out their
problem.

9. When kids are angry, it is best to:

- Take a deep _____.

- Raise your hand.

- Talk with the teacher and try to work out the problem.

10. Teachers and parents want to _____, especially when
students are angry.

11. Talking with an adult is a _____ way to feel better when
we're angry.

WORD BOX

hurt	everybody	smart
feel	breath	stomach
choice	teacher	rules
angry	help	

QUEST Program I UPDATE!

Dear Parent,

Your child has been working hard in QUEST Program I this week to learn and practice social skills. The story we read to introduce our new skill was called:

Everybody Gets Angry Sometimes

Together we have learned:

- All adults and children get angry sometimes.

- Shutting down or becoming aggressive when we are angry is not a good choice.

- When kids feel angry at school, they should:

  - Take a deep breath.
  - Raise their hand.
  - Talk about it with their teacher.

You can help your child practice at home by:

- Modeling healthy anger/stress management by taking breaks when you are upset, taking a deep breath, and talking over problems when calm.

- Reminding your child about anger management steps when you anticipate they may experience challenging events.

  e.g., "Stan, I know it's hard for you to wait in that long line at the bank, so remember to take some deep breaths that will help you feel better!"

  "Last time we went to the dentist, you were very angry. Let's talk about tomorrow's visit now and see if we can figure out ways to make it better."

Thanks for your help!

Comforting Others - Story 4-5

Everybody gets sad and angry sometimes. Some people like to be alone when they feel sad or angry. Other people like to talk about their problems. Most adults and kids like to be helpful when they see someone who is sad or angry.

One way to be helpful when we see a friend who is sad or angry is to comfort them. Comforting someone means doing things to make them feel better. Usually friends comfort each other by:

- Listening;
- Nodding;
- Talking about the problem;
- Getting an adult if our friend needs more help.

Kids and even adults can't always make problems go away, but friends can let each other know that they care by comforting each other when they feel sad or angry. When we comfort people, they may feel better. Sometimes adults or friends might also try to comfort us when we are sad or angry. This is one way people show they care.

I can tell friends and adults when I feel sad or angry. I can comfort my family and friends when they are sad and angry by listening, nodding, and talking about the problem. I can get an adult if my friend needs more help. I can let my family and friends comfort me too. This is a way people show they care about each other.

Comforting Others - Activity Sheet 4-5

Name _____

1. Find these words or phrases in the story and highlight them:

   helpful   adults   listening

   talk   problem   comfort

2. Think about a time you needed comforting because you were
   sad. Draw a picture of something or someone who made you feel
   better. Tell the class about your picture.

Comforting Others - Activity Sheet 4-5

Materials

- "Comforting Others" scenario cards

- "Comforting Others" game board

Procedure

- Prior to class, cut out the "Comforting Others" scenario cards.

- Place the "Comforting Others" scenario cards on the game board.

- Ask each student to take turns picking a "Comforting Others" scenario card, read it out loud, and place card on the game board in the location that applies to what action they would take to offer comfort for that situation.

Give a hug

Leave the
person alone

Comforting
Others -
Game 4-5

Place cards here

Ask if you
can help

Go and get
an adult

Comforting Others - Scenario Cards 4-5

Your grandmother
is crying.

Your teacher falls on
the floor in math class.

In the lunchroom,
you see a student
crying, but a teacher
is helping.

Your friend tells you
that she is really
worried about the
school trip.

Two boys are
yelling at each other
in the bathroom.

Another student
drops their books
in the hall.

Your teacher says "She
will be out for a month
because she is having
an operation."

A girl you don't know
is sitting all alone on
the playground.

Comforting Others - Scenario Cards 4-5

Your dad tells you that he lost his best watch.

Your brother falls down outside.

Your mother has her head down on the kitchen table.

A boy at school is trying to get his locker open, but can't do it.

Another student shows you that she cut her knee.

A student comes to school in a wheelchair.

Your cousin didn't make the baseball team.

Your aunt burns her hand on the stove.

QUEST Program I Social Skills Curriculum for Elementary School Students with Autism
© by JoEllen Cumpata and Susan Fell. Future Horizons, Inc.

Comforting Others - Report 4-5

Names_____

Date_____

Directions: Read the sentences below. Fill in the blanks for each question. Look at the story or use the word box if you need help.

1. _____ gets sad and angry sometimes.

2. Some people like to be alone when they feel sad or angry, and other people like to talk about their _____.

3. Most adults and kids like to be _____ when they see someone who is sad or angry.

4. One way to be helpful when we see a friend who is sad or angry is to _____them.

5. Comforting someone means doing things to make them feel _____.

6. Usually friends comfort each other by:

    a. Listening;

    b. Nodding;

c. _____ about the problem;

d. Getting an _____ if our friend needs more help.

7. Kids and even adults can't always make problems go
_____.

8. But friends can let each other know that they _____ by comforting each other when they feel sad or angry.

9. When we comfort _____, they may feel better.

WORD BOX

better	adult	helpful
Everybody	Talking	away
comfort	others	care
problems		

QUEST Program I UPDATE!

Dear Parent,

Your child has been working hard in QUEST Program I this week to learn and practice social skills. The story we read to introduce our new skill was called:

Comforting Others

Together we have learned:

- It is nice to be helpful when someone feels bad.

- We can be helpful by:

  - Listening;
  - Nodding;
  - Talking with them about the problem;
  - Getting an adult if our friend needs more help.

You can help your child practice at home by:

- Being a good role model by listening, nodding, and talking with those who you care about when they are in need.

- Assisting your child as they attempt to comfort others.

  e.g., "I see your sister is upset that she can't go to the party. Why don't you see if she wants to go to the park with us."

  "Dad's really upset tonight about Grandma. I'm sure he would feel better if you went and gave him a hug."

Thanks for your help!

QUEST Program I Parent/Teacher Evaluation
Unit 4 - Everybody Has Feelings

Student Name _____   Date _____

Parent/Teacher Name _____

We have just completed a unit in QUEST Program I, Everybody Has Feelings. Please fill out the rating scale below to assist us in determining how well your student has generalized the skills taught and if you have noticed improvement in their level of skill over the past six weeks. Check all boxes which apply below.

Skill	Does Independently	Does Only With Adult Reminders	Improvement Noted (Post-test only)
I Have Feelings: Identifying correct feelings in self and others.			
Telling People How I Feel: Using words to express feelings.			
Faces and Bodies Can Talk: Recognizing and responding appropriately to body language in others, using body language appropriately for own emotions.			
Everybody Gets Angry Sometimes: Expressing in words when angry, frustrated, or annoyed. Availing self to discussion about problem solving when upset.			
Comforting Others: Attempting to comfort those in need by asking if they can help. Using hugs/kisses appropriately with family and knows when to get adult help if others have a problem.			

Comments_____

_____

Thank you for your input!

QUEST Program I Social Skills Curriculum for Elementary School Students with Autism
© by JoEllen Cumpata and Susan Fell. Future Horizons, Inc.

Unit 5

Being Safe

Goal and Objectives Unit 5 - Being Safe

Goal

To become more aware of personal safety concerns and strategies.

Objectives

➢ To know what to do at home if there is a problem or home emergency.

➢ To learn the difference between friends and strangers and know how to respond if approached by an unknown adult.

➢ To learn steps to follow during a school or family outing.

➢ To identify basic safety signs.

➢ To practice safe use of technology.

Stories, Activities, and Parent Updates

Stories can be read by parents, teachers, or students. Often students gain a deeper under-standing of skills when stories are discussed in detail in a group setting. Asking students to summarize paragraphs, relate their personal experiences, and complete activities are all effective ways to increase generalization of skills. Parent Updates provide additional ways to continue learning at home.

Topics included in this unit are:

1. Being Safe at Home

2. Meeting New People

3. Leaving School with My Class

4. Watching for Safety Signs

5. Technology Safety

Being Safe at Home - Story 5-1

When kids are small, grown-ups make sure they are safe at home. When kids get older, they need to learn how to stay safe when their parents are busy or when someone else is taking care of them.

When kids are at home, they might play video games. When kids are at home, they might read or do homework. When kids are at home, they might make a snack. When kids are at home, they might take a bath or shower. When kids are at home, they need to be safe.

Sometimes problems happen at home. When problems happen, it is good to know what to do. Most families talk about what is safe and what is dangerous. Most families talk about rules that keep us safe. Families also talk about what to do if there is a problem or an emergency.

If there is a problem at home, usually grown-ups can decide how and when to fix it. If there is an emergency at home, it is important to call 911 so doctors, police, or fire fighters can help. Kids NEVER call 911 if the problem can be fixed or if no one is in danger. Calling 911 is JUST for emergencies.

An emergency is a problem that is or gets dangerous. An emergency might be when someone gets hurt. An emergency might be when something is on fire. An emergency might be when someone is in danger.

Talking with adults at home is the best way to know what to do when there is a problem or an emergency. Sometimes kids write down information on a Home Safety List and put it on the refrigerator. When there is a Home Safety List on the refrigerator, kids and grown-ups know what to do and can stay safe.

I can talk with my parents about what to do if there is a problem or an emergency. I can make a Home Safety List and put it on my refrigerator then I will know what to do if there is a problem or an emergency.

Being Safe at Home - Activity Sheet - 5-1

Name _____

1. Find these words or phrases in the story and highlight them:

   Home   dangerous   problems

   adults   safe   emergency

2. The pictures below show things that might happen at home. Tell a story about one of the pictures below. Decide if you would call 911 for each picture.

Let's Talk About Safety - Handout 5-1

Name _____

Directions: Talk with your parents about the rules at your house and ways to be safe. Circle the things below that you can do at home and write any special rules in the box. Complete your "Let's Talk About Safety" handout and bring it back to QUEST I class.

When I am at home alone, I am allowed to

Play in the yard	Answer the door	Watch TV

Have a friend over	Use the telephone	Make food

Use the computer	Leave the house	Take a shower or bath

I can call these people if I need help at home:

Name _____   Phone _____

Name _____   Phone _____

Home Safety List - Rules 5-1

My address is:_____

_____

When I need help, I can call

Police/Fire: 911 (ONLY IF THERE IS AN EMERGENCY!)_____

_____

_____

My safety rules:

1. _____

2. _____

3. _____

4. _____

5. _____

Being Safe at Home - Report 5-1

Names_____

Date_____

Directions: Read the sentences below. Fill in the blanks for each question. Look at the story or use the word box if you need help.

1. When kids are small, grown-ups make sure they are _____ at home.

2. When kids get older, they need to _____ how to stay safe when their parents are busy or when someone else is taking care of them.

3. When kids are at home, they might play a _____ _____, read, do homework, or make a snack.

4. Sometimes _____ happen at home.

5. Most families talk about what is safe and what is _____.

6. Most families talk about _____ that keep us safe.

7. If there is a problem at home, usually grown-ups will _____ how and when to fix it.

QUEST Program I Social Skills Curriculum for Elementary School Students with Autism
© by JoEllen Cumpata and Susan Fell. Future Horizons, Inc.

8. If there is an emergency at home, it is important to call 911, but NEVER call 911 if the problem can be _____, or if no one is in danger.

9. _____ with adults at home is the best way to know what to do when there is a problem or an emergency.

10. When there is a Home _____ List on the refrigerator kids and grown-ups know what to do and can stay safe.

WORD BOX

rules	learn	dangerous
decide	safe	Safety
video game	Talking	problems
fixed		

QUEST Program I UPDATE!

Dear Parent,

Your child has been working hard in QUEST Program I this week to learn and practice social skills. The story we read to introduce our new skill was called:

Being Safe at Home

Together we have learned:

- Students must start thinking about ways to be safe.

- Parents have different rules about home safety.

- Calling 911 is for emergencies only, not problems that can be fixed.

- It's a good idea to talk with parents and develop a Home Safety List to remember home safety rules.

You can help your child practice at home by:

- Discussing and helping your child complete their "Let's Talk About Safety" handout.

- Encouraging family discussions and questions regarding home safety.

  e.g., "If I were in the shower and someone came to the door who you did not know, what would you do?"
  "If you broke something that was made of glass, what would you do?"
  "If I were to fall and hurt myself, who could you call?"
  "Show me how you use the microwave."

Thanks for your help!

Meeting New People - Story 5-2

It's fun to meet new people. Sometimes we meet new people at school. We meet new teachers and new students on the first day of school. We meet new kids who come to our school during the school year. We meet substitute teachers when our teacher is out.

Sometimes we meet new people at home. We might meet new people who work with our parents. We might meet kids who are friends with our brothers or sisters. We might meet new neighbors. We might meet relatives whom we have never met before.

Meeting new people is okay as long as our teachers or parents know who the person is. Our teachers and parents know when new people are safe. Our teachers and parents also know which new people might not be safe. If our teachers or parents don't know who the new person is, then he or she is a stranger.

Some strangers try to get to know kids, so they can do things that are bad. Some strangers try to get to know kids, so they can hurt them. Some strangers try to get to know kids, so they can take things from them. These people are not friendly and might be dangerous.

Kids should NEVER go anywhere with a stranger unless their parent or teacher says "It is okay." If kids see a stranger who wants them to come closer, talk, or get in his car, kids should say "NO!" and run away.

Asking your parents and teachers if you can talk with new people is smart. Staying away from strangers, unless your parents or teachers say "It's okay" is a good idea. Talking with your parents or teachers about strangers and new people is one way to be safe.

Meeting New People - Activity Sheet 5-2

Name _____

1. Find these words or phrases in the story and highlight them:

friends	safe	strangers
never	new	school

2. Read the people below. Put an 'X' over people who are strangers.

Your school principal.

A woman standing in line at the grocery store.

Your grandmother.

Your math teacher.

The mail carrier.

A new neighbor your family hasn't met yet.

Your babysitter.

Your dentist.

A person selling magazines who is knocking at your door.

A man mowing your neighbor's lawn.

A substitute teacher.

A woman walking her dog at the park.

Meeting New People - Report 5-2

Names_____

Date_____

Directions: Read the sentences below. Fill in the blanks for each question. Look at the story or use the word box if you need help.

1. It's fun to meet_____ people.

2. We meet new teachers and new _____ on the first day of school.

3. We _____ new kids who come to our school during the school year.

4. We might meet kids who are friends with our brothers or sisters or new _____.

5. Meeting new people is _____ as long as our teachers or parents know who the person is.

6. Our teachers and parents know which new people are _____, and which new people might not be safe.

7. If our teachers or parents don't know who the new person is, then they are a _____.

8. Some strangers try to get to know kids, so they can do things that are bad, take things from them, or try to _____ them.

9. These people are not friendly and might be _____.

10. Kids should _____ go anywhere with a stranger unless their parent or teacher says "It is okay."

11. If kids see a stranger who wants them to come closer, talk, or get in his car, kids should say _____ and run away.

WORD BOX

never	neighbors	hurt
okay	new	students
stranger	meet	"NO!"
safe	dangerous	

QUEST Program I UPDATE!

Dear Parent,

Your child has been working hard in QUEST Program I this week to learn and practice social skills. The story we read to introduce our new skill was called:

Meeting New People

Together we have learned:

- Meeting new people is a normal part of daily life.

- Parents or teachers will assist students in determining which strangers are safe.

- Students should never go anywhere with a stranger or new person unless their parent or teacher has specifically told them to.

You can help your child practice at home by:

- Remind your child often that they are never to speak to a stranger in person or online unless you or their teacher has given the okay.

- Identify "safe" people who may care for or call your child if you are unavailable.

  e.g., "If I am tied up at work and unable to pick you up from school, the only people who might come to get you would be ... "

Thanks for your help!

Leaving School with My Class - Story 5-3

Sometimes I go on a family trip. Sometimes I go on a school trip. I can have fun on a family trip. I can have fun on a school trip. I can have fun when I'm away from home.

When I'm away from home, I need to be safe. When I'm on a school trip, I need to stay close to my group and follow the rules. If I stay close to my group and follow the rules, I will be safe.

Sometimes when kids are on a school or family trip, they don't stay close to the group. Sometimes students can't find their group, this can feel scary. If kids know what to do when they are lost, it's not so scary. When kids can't find their group, they need to be calm and smart.

If kids can't find their group, they should do three things:

1. STAND STILL and let their group find them. Sometimes when kids are lost, they run around looking for their group, this isn't smart. If kids stand still for five to ten minutes, their group can find them.

2. CALL your parent or teacher. If you have your cell phone, call your parent or teacher and let them know you can't find the group. They will tell you to stand still, so the group can find you.

3. FIND A HELPFUL PERSON. You can look for a helpful person if you don't have a phone and you've waited for five to ten minutes. A helpful person is someone taking care of children, wearing a uniform or nametag, or working at a cash register. You can tell the helpful person you are lost and they will help.

I can have fun when I go on a school trip. I can have fun when I go on a family trip. I can be safe when I follow the rules and stay close to the group. If I get lost, I can wait, call, or find a helpful person.

QUEST Program I Social Skills Curriculum for Elementary School Students with Autism
© by JoEllen Cumpata and Susan Fell. Future Horizons, Inc.

Help I'm Lost! - Rules 5-3

1. Stay in the same spot for five to ten minutes.

2. Call your parent, a family member, or friend if you have a cell phone.

3. Find a helpful person.

- Someone with children

- Someone wearing a uniform or nametag

- Someone working at a cash register

4. Tell them you are lost.

Leaving School with My Class -
Activity Sheet 5-3

Name _____

1. Find these words or phrases in the story and highlight them:

   helpful   calm   smart

   wait   group   safe

2. Look at the pictures below. Tell a story about how this student got lost and what they did, so they could be back with their group.

Leaving School with My Class - Report 5-3

Names_____

Date_____

Directions: Read the sentences below. Fill in the blanks for each question.
Look at the story or use the word box if you need help.

1. Sometimes I go on a _____ trip.

2. Sometimes I go on a school _____.

3. I can have _____when I'm away from home.

4. When I'm away from home, I need to be _____.

5. When I'm on a school trip, I need to stay _____ to my group.

6. If I stay close to my group and follow the _____, I will be safe.

7. If I can't find my group, I should do three things:

   • _____ _____for five to ten minutes and let my
     group find me.

   • Call my parent or _____ if I have my cell phone.

   • Find a _____ person who is wearing a uniform or
     nametag, working at a cash register, or taking care of children.

WORD BOX

Stand still	trip	family
helpful	fun	safe
close	teacher	rules

QUEST Program I Social Skills Curriculum for Elementary School Students with Autism

QUEST Program I UPDATE!

Dear Parent,

Your child has been working hard in QUEST Program I this week to learn and practice social skills. The story we read to introduce our new skill was called:

Leaving School with My Class

Together we have learned:

- Three steps to follow if separated from your group.
- Who "helpful people" are in cities, shops, museums, parks, and recreational areas.
- How to approach a "helpful person" to get assistance.

You can help your child practice at home by:

- Discussing the safety strategies below with your child before school field trips or family outings:

    1. **Stay in the same place for five to ten minutes** – Usually people from the group will come looking for a student as soon as they notice that the student is missing.
    2. **Use your cell phone to call a parent or family member.**
    3. **Find a helpful person** – When students are inside a building, helpful people are often employees who work in the building. They might be working a cash register, taking admission tickets, or sitting behind a desk. When students are outside, helpful people are usually in an office building, in the park, or recreational area. Sometimes helpful people wear uniforms like policemen, camp rangers, or store security personnel.
    4. **Let the helpful person know you are separated from your group** – Helpful people will usually have some way of finding a group of people. Sometimes they will use a loudspeaker or telephone to find a student's group.

Thanks for your help!

Watching for Safety Signs - Story 5-4

When kids are out in the community or away from home, it is important to be safe. One way kids can be safe is to look for safety signs. Most safety signs are red, orange, or yellow. Safety signs give us information about ways to be safe.

The EXIT sign is one safety sign. EXIT signs are turned on. EXIT signs are red and white. EXIT signs are usually above doors and show us which way to get out of a building. If kids need to get out of a building, they should look for an EXIT sign.

Another safety sign is the WALK/DON'T WALK sign. The WALK/DON'T WALK sign tells us when it is okay to cross a busy street. Drivers know to stop when the light is red. When the light is red, the WALK sign is on for people crossing the street. When drivers see a green light, they keep driving, and the DON'T WALK sign comes on. When the DON'T WALK sign is on, it is NOT SAFE to cross the street.

QUEST Program I Social Skills Curriculum for Elementary School Students with Autism
© by JoEllen Cumpata and Susan Fell. Future Horizons, Inc.

If kids see a sign that says DANGER or KEEP OUT, it is important that they stay away. DAN-GER or KEEP OUT signs are put in places where people can get hurt.

Sometimes kids don't know what signs mean. If kids don't know what a sign means, it is smart to ask. Most signs are important and give us information that helps us stay safe. Asking a parent, teacher, or another helpful adult what a sign means helps to keep us safe.

Safety signs are inside and outside. Safety signs give kids important information about ways to stay safe. I can watch for safety signs when I'm in a building or outside. When I follow safety signs, I can stay safe.

Watching for Safety Signs - Activity Sheet 5-4

Name _____

1. Find these words or phrases in the story and highlight them:

smart	safety	EXIT
signs	ask	look

2. Look at the safety signs below and talk about what they mean. If you don't know what a sign means, ask your teacher.

Watching for Safety Signs - Report 5-4

Names_____

Date _____

Directions: Read the sentences below. Fill in the blanks for each question. Look at the story or use the word box if you need help.

1. When kids are out in the _____or away from home, it is important to be safe.

2. One way kids can be safe is to look for safety _____.

3. Safety signs give us _____about ways to be safe.

4. EXIT signs are usually above _____and show us which way to get out of a building.

5. The WALK/DON'T WALK sign tells kids when it is okay to _____ a busy street.

6. If kids see a sign that says DANGER or KEEP OUT, it is important that they _____ _____, because if they go near, they can get hurt.

7. If kids don't know what a sign means, it is _____ to ask their parent or teacher.

8. Most signs are important and give us information to help us stay
   _____.

9. I can _____ for safety signs when I'm in a building or
   outside.

WORD BOX

cross	safe	signs
community	smart	stay away
watch	information	doors

QUEST Program I UPDATE!

Dear Parent,

Your child has been working hard in QUEST Program I this week to learn and practice social skills. The story we read to introduce our new skill was called:

Watching for Safety Signs

Together we have learned:

- Why it is important to watch for safety signs.

- What basic safety signs mean (Exit, Walk/Don't Walk, Danger, Keep Out, etc.).

You can help your child practice at home by:

- Pointing out safety signs in your community.

- Discussing the meaning of safety signs with your child.

- Being a good role model for your child by following safety signs at all times, even when it's not convenient.

  e.g., "Yes I know we can cross the street here, but it is safer to walk down to the light to cross."

Thanks for your help!

Technology Safety - Story 5-5

It's fun to use computers, phones, and other kinds of technology. Kids use technology every day. Kids use technology to play games. Kids use technology to learn. Kids use technology to talk to other kids.

Using technology can be fun, but it can also be dangerous. Using technology can even get kids in trouble. Kids need to follow safety rules when they use technology. When kids follow safety rules, they can have fun and stay safe.

Kids should NEVER talk with strangers on their phone or computer. Strangers are people your parents or teachers don't know. Talking with strangers is dangerous and might get kids in trouble. If a stranger calls, texts, or sends a message, kids should always tell an adult right away!

One important technology safety rule is about personal information. Kids should NEVER give out personal information unless their parent or teacher says it's okay. Personal information means your:

- name
- phone number
- address
- birth date
- name of your school

Strangers who try to get to know kids on the computer or phone can be dangerous. Some people want to get personal information from kids, so they can hurt them. Some people want to get personal information from kids, so they can steal things from them. Some people want to get personal information from kids, so they can break the law.

I can stay safe when I use technology. I can stay safe by not talking to strangers on my computer or phone. I can stay safe when I don't give out any of my personal information on my phone or computer. When I use technology safety rules, I can have fun and be safe.

Technology Safety - Activity Sheet 5-5

Name _____

1. Find these words or phrases in the story and highlight them:

   safety   technology   computers

   rules   personal   fun
                         information

2. Write types of personal information that kids should NEVER give
   to a stranger on their phone or computer.

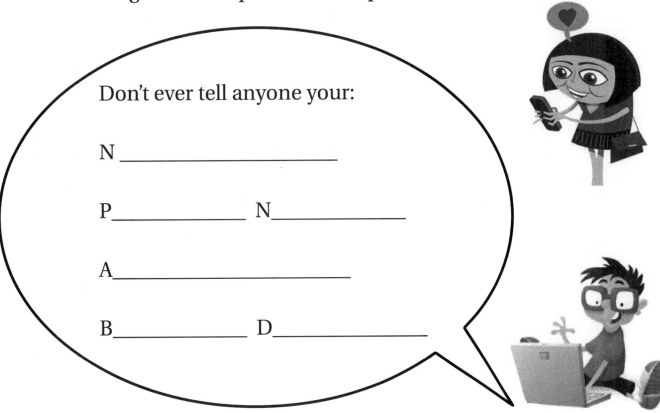

Don't ever tell anyone your:

N _____

P_____ N_____

A_____

B_____ D_____

Technology Safety - Report 5-5

Names_____

Date_____

Directions: Read the sentences below. Fill in the blanks for each question. Look at the story or use the word box if you need help.

1. It's fun to use computers, phones, and other kinds of

    _____.

2. Kids use technology to play games, to learn, and to _____ to other kids.

3. Using technology can be fun, but it can also be _____.

4. Using technology can even get kids in _____.

5. Kids need to follow _____ _____ when they use technology.

6. When kids follow safety rules, they can have fun and stay

    _____.

7. Kids should never talk with _____ on their phone or computer.

8. If a stranger calls, texts, or sends a message, kids should always tell an _____ RIGHT AWAY!

9. Kids should NEVER give out personal information like their name, phone number, or _____ unless their parent or teacher says "It's Okay."

WORD BOX

safe	adult	dangerous
strangers	talk	address
technology	trouble	safety rules

QUEST Program I UPDATE!

Dear Parent,

Your child has been working hard in QUEST Program I this week to learn and practice social skills. The story we read to introduce our new skill was called:

Technology Safety

Together we have learned:

- The importance of being safe when using technology.

- Why communicating with strangers online is dangerous.

- What personal information is and why it is dangerous to share this information with others on the computer.

You can help your child practice at home by:

- Discussing your own home computer safety rules, especially regarding personal information, video journals, and diaries.

- Reviewing what personal information is and talking to your child about why it is dangerous to share this information with others on the computer.

Thanks for your help!

QUEST Program I Parent/Teacher Evaluation
Unit 5 - Personal Safety

Student Name _____ Date _____

Parent/Teacher Name _____

We have just completed a unit in QUEST Program I on Personal Safety. Please fill out the rating scale below to assist us in determining how well your student has generalized the skills taught and if you have noticed improvement in their level of skill over the past six weeks. Check all boxes which apply below.

Skill	Does Independently	Does Only With Adult Reminders	Improvement Noted (Post-test only)
Being Safe at Home: Understanding when to call 911 and when to wait for adult help, how to safely prepare food, who to allow into the home.			
Meeting New People: Showing ease with meeting new people, distinguishing safe and dangerous strangers, understanding what to do if approached by a stranger.			
Leaving School with My Class: Comfortably participates in school trips by following directions and understanding what to do if lost.			
Watching for Safety Signs: Looking for and use safety signs when in the community without adult reminders (Walk/Won't Walk, Keep Out, EXIT, etc.).			
Technology Safety: Understanding that some computer use can be dangerous. Understanding what personal information is and does not disclose without adult permission, consults parent/teacher when technology questions arise.			

Comments_____

_____

Thank you for your input!

Unit 6

Being Responsible

Goal and Objectives Unit 6 - Being Responsible

Goal

To understand the concept of responsibility and practice ways to show respect for self and others.

Objectives

➤ To learn about the concept of rules and appreciate the concept of personal space and the belongings of others.

➤ To understand and practice ways to show appreciation and the concepts of sharing, waiting, and remaining quiet when asked.

➤ To gain an appreciation for differences in parenting and teaching styles, respond appropriately to authority figures, and learn effective and acceptable ways to clarify adult expectations.

➤ To understand the concept of cooperation and practice three useful steps when disagreements occur.

➤ To identify appropriate times and ways to request adult assistance.

Stories, Activities, and Parent Updates

Stories can be read by parents, teachers, or students. Often students gain a deeper understanding of skills when stories are discussed in detail in a group setting. Asking students to summarize paragraphs, relate their personal experiences, and complete activities are all effective ways to increase generalization of skills. Parent Updates provide additional ways to continue learning at home.

Topics included in this unit are:

1. Being Respectful of Others

2. Using Good Manners

3. Correcting Adults

4. Cooperating

5. When I Need Help

Being Respectful of Others - Story 6-1

Everyone has rules. Families have rules at home. Principals, teachers, and students have rules at school. Rules help people respect each other. Respect means treating other people the same way you want them to treat you—with kindness.

Kids usually have things that belong to them. Most kids have things that belong to them at home. Kids have things that belong to them at school too. Sometimes kids share, sometimes they don't.

At school, students usually have pencils, paper, and other things that belong to them. Sometimes students have a desk, table, or locker where they can keep their things. Teachers also have things at school that belong to them. Some supplies are shared at school and are there for everyone. Other things belong only to one student or teacher and are not shared without permission.

School rules usually say that kids cannot touch things that don't belong to them. This is one way we can be respectful and get along. Sometimes kids see something interesting or fun that doesn't belong to them and they want to take a closer look. It is okay to be interested, but before touching anything that doesn't belong to them, kids MUST ask permission.

I can follow school rules. I can be respectful of other people by asking before I touch their things. I can wait until I have permission to touch things that don't belong to me.

Being Respectful of Others - Activity Sheet 6-1

Name _____

1. Find these words or phrases in the story and highlight them:

   respect   supplies   touch

   belong   rules   share

2. Circle the items below that everyone can use. Put an 'X' through the items that you must ask permission to touch.

Being Respectful of Others - Activity Sheet 6-1

Materials

- Being Respectful of Others story

- Being Respectful of Others poster

- Personal/Shared Items cards

Procedure

- Prior to class, cut out "Personal/Shared Items" cards and place on table.

- Read "Being Respectful of Others" story aloud in class and discuss.

- Display "Being Respectful of Others" poster in the room.

- Place Personal/Shared Items cards on the table.

- Ask one student to choose an item and decide if it is a shared item in the classroom or a personal item.

- Ask the student to place it in the correct location on the poster.

- If the item is a personal item, ask the students to volunteer ways they could ask to use the item in a respectful way.

Being Respectful of Others! - Poster 6-1

This is a personal item.

Ask permission before touching.

This is a shared item.

Everyone can use.

Remember successful students treat others with kindness and respect!

Personal/Shared Items - Cards 6-1

QUEST Program I Social Skills Curriculum for Elementary School Students with Autism

Personal/Shared Items - Cards 6-1

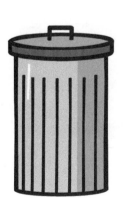

Personal/Shared Items - Cards 6-1

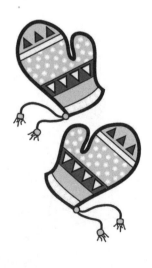

Being Respectful of Others - Report 6-1

Names_____

Date_____

Directions: Read the sentences below. Fill in the blanks for each question. Look at the story or use the word box if you need help.

1. Everyone has _____.

2. Principals, teachers, and _____ have rules at school.

3. Rules help people _____each other.

4. Respect means treating other people the _____ _____ you want them to treat you, with kindness.

5. Kids usually have things that _____ to them.

6. Sometimes kids _____, sometimes they don't.

7. Some _____ are shared at school and are there for everyone.

8. Other things belong only to one student or teacher and are not shared without _____.

9. School rules usually say that kids cannot _____ things that don't belong to them.

10. _____touching anything that doesn't belong to them, kids MUST ask permission.

WORD BOX

permission	belong	rules
Before	students	share
supplies	same way	respect
touch		

QUEST Program I UPDATE!

Dear Parent,

Your child has been working hard in QUEST Program I this week to learn and practice social skills. The story we read to introduce our new skill was called:

Being Respectful of Others

Together we have learned:

- Why rules are important.

- The definition of respect.

- Why some things at school are shared while others are not.

You can help your child practice at home by:

- Modeling respect for your family member's personal items and space.

  e.g., "Karen, I need to take several files to the library, could I borrow your backpack today?"

  "Andrew, your new video game is so much fun, could Sam try it when he comes over today?"

- Calmly reminding your child when they are disrespectful.

  e.g., "I felt so angry when my new markers were left open. Please ask before you borrow my things next time."

  "Eric, I'm talking with Aunt Sue right now. Sit in the living room and I will answer your question when I'm done."

Thanks for your help!

Using Good Manners - Story 6-2

When children are tiny, their parents usually teach them good manners. This means saying please and thank you, waiting patiently, sharing, and being quiet when asked. In school, manners are important too.

Using manners at school helps people get along and have a good day. Students need to remember to say "Please" when they want assistance or if they are asking for something. Saying "Thank you" when someone is helpful or kind is one way students let others know that we have good manners.

When students wait their turn without pushing or yelling, everyone feels calm and happy. If kids push or yell instead of waiting quietly, it makes others angry. Angry people make everyone feel uncomfortable.

Sharing and listening to others help students make friends and have fun. Students share school supplies, games, and sometimes even food. Listening to teachers, other students, and parents when they are talking is one way to use good manners.

When students feel excited, angry, or sad, they sometimes forget about manners. Teachers and other adults will often remind students to wait, be quiet, or share when they forget. Some students forget about manners and need reminders. It is okay to forget sometimes.

I can follow school rules and get along with others by using manners. I can remember to wait, listen, say "Please" and Thank you," and respect others in school. When I forget, it is okay for my teacher to give me a reminder. I can help make school a calm and fun place when I use my manners.

Using Good Manners - Activity Sheet 6-2

Name _____

1. Find these words or phrases in the story and **highlight them:**

   turn   manners   **listening**

   thank you   sharing   **forget**

2. Look at the pictures below. Tell a story about how **good manners** might come in handy in each situation.

Using Good Manners - Activity Sheet 6-2

Materials

- Using Good Manners story

Procedure

- Prior to class, cut out the "Using Good Manners" scenario cards.

- Read "Using Good Manners" story aloud in class and discuss.

- Place "Using Good Manners" Manners Detective game board on the table.

- Place "Using Good Manners" scenario cards in the center of the board.

- Ask a student to choose a card, read it aloud, and determine which good manners rule has been broken.

- Ask the student to place the card on the correct corner of the game board.

- Ask the student to share how manners could correct the situation.

- Continue play until all students have had a turn.

QUEST Program I Social Skills Curriculum for Elementary School Students with Autism
© by JoEllen Cumpata and Susan Fell. Future Horizons, Inc.

Forgot to say "Please" or "Thank you."

Forgot to listen.

Using Good Manners - Manners Detective Board Game 6-2

Place cards here

Forgot to wait for their turn.

Forgot to respect others' things.

Using Good Manners - Scenario Cards 6-2

Pam is really thirsty, so she pushes Sam out of line to get a drink.

Joey needs a pencil, so he takes one he sees on the teacher's desk.

Brian has four cookies at lunch and gives one to Nick. Nick says nothing.

Ellen brings cupcakes to school for her birthday. Ruth takes one and says, "Yum!"

Mrs. Smith is talking to her students about their spelling words. Jane and Eric are whispering.

In math class, Jessie always shouts out the answer without raising his hand.

The principal announces a special guest is coming. Brett is laying his head on his desk.

Chris offers to help Mark practice catching the football. Mark says, "Okay."

Using Good Manners - Scenario Cards 6-2

Sarah really likes Emily's lunchbox. Sarah sees it in the lost and found and she takes it home.

Andrew leaves his hat in Erin's car. She gives it back to him at school. Andrew throws it in his backpack and walks away.

John is playing with his handheld video game. Craig grabs it from him and says "Let me play!"

A group of kids are playing with a ball after school. Tracy takes it because she wants to play.

The bathroom line is really long. Erica tells Anna if she doesn't let her cut she won't be her friend.

Jane is the only one who doesn't have markers. She takes some from the art room when the teacher isn't looking.

Joey usually talks about boring things, so Claire interrupts him a lot.

Eric thinks hiding Brian's lunch money is funny.

Using Good Manners - Report 6-2

Names_____

Date _____

Directions: Read the sentences below. Fill in the blanks for each question. Look at the story or use the word box if you need help.

1. When children are tiny, their parents usually teach them good
   _____.

2. This means saying "Please" and "Thank-you," waiting
   _____, sharing, and being quiet when asked.

3. Using manners at _____ helps people get along and
   have a good day.

4. Students need to remember to say _____ when they
   want assistance or if they are asking for something.

5. Saying "Thank you" when someone is _____ or kind is
   one way students let others know that we have good manners.

6. When students _____ their turn without pushing or
   yelling, everyone feels calm and happy.

7. If kids push or yell instead of waiting quietly, it makes others
   _____ and uncomfortable.

QUEST Program I Social Skills Curriculum for Elementary School Students with Autism
© by JoEllen Cumpata and Susan Fell. Future Horizons, Inc.

8. Sharing and listening to others helps students make
_____ and have fun.

9. Sometimes kids _____, so teachers and other adults
will often remind students to use their manners.

WORD BOX

wait	"Please"	patiently
manners	helpful	forget
school	angry	friends

QUEST Program I UPDATE!

Dear Parent,

Your child has been working hard in QUEST Program I this week to learn and practice social skills. The story we read to introduce our new skill was called:

Using Good Manners

Together we have learned:

- Why using good manners help people get along.

- The importance of listening, waiting your turn, saying "Please" and "Thank you," and respecting others' property.

You can help your child practice at home by:

- Reminding your child about manners:

  e.g., "Polly, I know your Grandpa can talk for a long time, but he really likes it when we listen."

  "That was a really long line today at the toy store. You were so patient and waited your turn. What a grown-up thing to do!"

- Modeling good manners.

Thanks for your help!

Correcting Adults - Story 6-3

Families do things differently. Some families eat dinner at 5:00 p.m., and others eat at 8:00 p.m. Some families watch a lot of TV, and others watch very little. It is okay for families to have different rules, and it is okay for children to ask questions about the rules, but parents are always in charge of their children.

Teachers do things differently too. Some teachers like a very quiet classroom, and some don't mind a noisy classroom. Some teachers let students choose where they sit, and other teachers decide where students will sit. All adults are different. Teachers may talk with their students about the rules, but teachers are always responsible for deciding the rules in their classroom.

Children need to listen to parents and teachers, even when they do things a bit differently than someone else. Sometimes kids know that one teacher is doing things differently than another teacher, this is okay. People do things differently and have different rules. Students should not tell teachers that they are doing something wrong. It is okay for kids to ask parents or teachers questions if they don't understand the rules.

I can remember that teachers and parents are in charge. Teachers and parents may do things differently, and that is okay. If I don't understand a rule at home or school, I can ask questions.

Correcting Adults - Activity Sheet 6-3

Name _____

1. Find these words or phrases in the story and highlight them:

   rules   adults   wrong

   in charge   okay   different

2. Pretend you are the principal and design the rules for your school below:

My Perfect School

What time would school start and end?	What classes would be taught?
What would students wear?	**What food would be served in the cafeteria?**

QUEST Program I Social Skills Curriculum for Elementary School Students with Autism
© by JoEllen Cumpata and Susan Fell. Future Horizons, Inc.

Correcting Others - Report 6-3

Names_____

Date_____

Directions: Read the sentences below. Fill in the blanks for each question. Look at the story or use the word box if you need help.

1. Families do things _____.

2. It is okay for families to have different rules, and it is okay for children to ask _____ about the rules, but parents are always in charge of their children.

3. _____ do things differently too.

4. Teachers may talk with their students about the _____, but teachers are always responsible for deciding the rules in their classroom.

5. Children need to _____ to parents and teachers, even when they do things a bit differently than someone else.

6. People do things differently and have different rules, so _____should not tell teachers that they are doing something wrong.

7. It is _____ that students understand and follow the rules at school.

8. It is okay to ask parents or teachers questions if they don't _____ the rules.

9. I can remember that teachers and parents are in _____.

WORD BOX

questions	listen	understand
charge	teachers	rules
students	important	differently

QUEST Program I Social Skills Curriculum for Elementary School Students with Autism
© by JoEllen Cumpata and Susan Fell. Future Horizons, Inc.

QUEST Program I UPDATE!

Dear Parent,

Your child has been working hard in QUEST Program I this week to learn and practice social skills. The story we read to introduce our new skill was called:

Correcting Adults

Together we have learned:

- Families, teachers, and other adults have different rules.

- Children must listen and follow rules at home and school, even if they disagree.

You can help your child practice at home by:

- Reminding your child to be polite, even if they disagree with the rules.

  e.g., "I know you're not happy with our plans for this weekend, but I expect you to follow all of Grandma's rules when she is here, even if they are different from what we usually do."

  "Your substitute teacher has some different ways of doing things, and I know it is hard not to correct her, but you need to follow her rules while Mr. Smith is out sick, even if you don't like them."

Thanks for your help!

Cooperating - Story 6-4

School can be a fun and interesting place. Sometimes kids have disagreements. Kids might disagree about who goes first, what to do in class and on the playground, or even about what friends to play with. Disagreements happen to everyone, even adults.

Sometimes when kids have disagreements, they argue. This can make time at school uncomfortable. It is important for kids to learn how to cooperate with others when they are in school. Cooperating means talking about disagreements, being respectful, sharing things, listening, and working out solutions to problems.

When kids cooperate, they can learn more about other kids, work through arguments, and have a good day at school. When kids want to cooperate, they need to do the following:

- relax and take a breath;

- listen to the other student;

- talk about a way to solve the problem.

Sometimes when kids argue, they feel very angry and frustrated. When we are angry, it is hard to try to cooperate. If we are having a disagreement, it is smart to take a time out to calm down before trying to cooperate or get an adult to help talk things out. It is okay to wait to try to cooperate. Usually kids cooperate better when they are calm.

I can try to cooperate in school when I have a disagreement. I can relax, listen, and try to talk about ways to solve my problems. I can take some time to calm down when I'm angry and ask an adult to help. When I cooperate in school, I can have a fun and interesting day.

Cooperating - Activity Sheet 6-4

Name _____

1. Find these words or phrases in the story and highlight them:

   disagreements   argue   friends

   calm   solutions   listen

2. Look at the pictures below. Talk about what the children did and why they are not having a disagreement.

Cooperating - Report 6-4

Names_____

Date_____

Directions: Read the sentences below. Fill in the blanks for each question. Look at the story or use the word box if you need help.

1. School can be a fun and _____ place.

2. Sometimes kids have _____ about who goes first, what to do in class or on the playground, or even about what friends to play with.

3. Disagreements happen to _____, even adults.

4. Sometimes when kids have disagreements they _____ and it makes time at school uncomfortable.

5. It is important for kids to learn how to _____ with others when they are in school.

6. Cooperating means talking about disagreements, being _____, sharing things, listening, and working out solutions to problems.

7. When kids cooperate, they can _____ more about other kids, work through arguments, and have a good day at school.

8. When kids want to cooperate, they need to:

   - relax and take a _____;

   - listen to the other student;

   - talk about a way to solve the problem.

9. Sometimes when kids argue, they feel very _____ and frustrated, so it's hard to try to cooperate.

10. If we are having a disagreement, it is _____ to take a time out to calm down before trying to cooperate or get an adult to help talk things out.

11. It is okay to wait to try to cooperate, because kids cooperate better when they are _____.

WORD BOX

cooperate	angry	calm
breath	disagreements	argue
respectful	everyone	smart
learn	interesting	

QUEST Program I UPDATE!

Dear Parent,

Your child has been working hard in QUEST Program I this week to learn and practice social skills. The story we read to introduce our new skill was called:

Cooperating

Together we have learned:

- That all students have disagreements sometimes.

- That cooperating makes school more fun and interesting.

- The three steps students can use to cooperate.

    - Relax;

    - Listen;

    - Talk out the problem.

You can help your child practice at home by:

- Listening attentively to your child when disagreements occur.

- Encouraging cooperation at home.

    e.g.,   "Sam, I'm feeling a bit angry right now. I'm going to go to my room for 15 minutes, and then we can talk this out."

    "Wow, Julie, you really listened to Jessica when she was upset. That's a great way to solve problems!"

Thanks for your help!

When I Have a Problem - Story 6-5

Kids usually feel comfortable and happy in school, but sometimes they feel angry, sad, or frustrated. It is hard to listen, be respectful, use good manners, and cooperate when you feel sad, angry, or frustrated. Sometimes kids need help from an adult in school.

Adults in school are all there to be helpful. Principals, teachers, and classroom assistants are all ready to help students work through problems. Fighting and being disrespectful are against school rules and can get kids in trouble. Adults can help kids make good choices when they are angry, so they don't get in trouble.

Sometimes kids need to tell an adult about a problem before it becomes a fight. Kids are learning how to cooperate and get along, and they sometimes need adults to help. It is okay to tell an adult about problems in school or problems with other students.

If you feel sad, angry, or frustrated in class, you should:

- raise your hand;

- ask your teacher to talk in private;

- tell the teacher about the problem.

Teachers and principals are good problem solvers. They might talk about ways to solve the problem or talk with other students who were involved. Sometimes teachers might even make changes in the classroom, like moving a student's seat. Problem solving is one way teachers help kids have a fun and relaxing day.

I can ask for help in school when I feel sad, angry, or frustrated. I can raise my hand and talk with my teacher in a private place about my problem. I can get the help I need in school and have a fun and interesting day.

When I Have a Problem - Activity Sheet 6-5

Name _____

1. Find these words or phrases in the story and highlight them:

   frustrated   trouble   rules

   talk   problem   cooperate

2. Circle the things we *should* do when we have a problem at school. Put an 'X' over the things we *should NOT* do when we have a problem at school.

   Raise your hand   Throw your book

   Take a deep breath   Tell your teacher

   Hide in the bathroom   Cry about it

   Ask for a break   Yell at someone

When I Have a Problem - Activity Sheet 6-5

Materials –

- When I Have a Problem story

- Good Decision and Bad Decision cards for every student

- Good Decision/Bad Decision scenario cards

Procedure –

- Prior to class, cut out the "Good Decision/Bad Decision" scenario cards.

- Read "When I Have a Problem" story aloud in class and discuss.

- Give each child a "Good Decision" and a "Bad Decision" card.

- Place the "Good Decision/Bad Decision" scenario cards in the middle of the table face down.

- Choose a card and read aloud. Decide if the student on the card made a good or bad decision and hold up the correct card.

- Talk about other choices the student had in each situation.

Good Decision/Bad Decision - Cards 6-5

Good Decision!

Good Decision!

Good Decision/Bad Decision - Cards 6-5

Bad Decision!

Bad Decision!

Good Decision/Bad Decision - Scenario Cards 6-5

Cindy likes to jump rope on the playground. She tries to get a jump rope every day, but sometimes they're all gone before she can get one. This makes her very angry. Cindy usually shouts at the kids using the jump ropes and tries to pull them away.

Brad and Joey have been friends for a while, but lately Joey has been teasing Brad a lot. He tells him that he is getting fat and that he can't catch. Brad feels bad, but he doesn't know what to say to Joey. He decides to talk with his teacher about it after school.

Katie always pushes Sara out of the way to get in front of her in the lunch line. Sara is really getting frustrated! She decides today, when Katie gets in front of her, she will just push her back!

John doesn't understand the map project his teacher has just assigned. Everyone else seems to know what to do, and John is embarrassed to ask for help, so he decides to ask his best friend about it on their way home.

Good Decision/Bad Decision - Scenario Cards 6-5

All of Laura's friends get to ride together for the field trip, but Laura has to ride in Jack's car. Jack is really mean. Laura decides she will tell her mother she is sick on the day of the trip, so she doesn't have to go.

Most of the kids at school are nice, but Jeffrey is always mean. He calls kids' names, takes their things, and pushes a lot! Lilly tells Jeffrey that if he doesn't behave he is going to get into trouble!

Jack, Robbie, and Pete have been friends since kindergarten. A new kid started school this week, and he is always pulling Robbie away from Jack and Pete. Jack decides to tell his teacher.

Carrie likes to sit alone in the corner near the window and the big blue pillow when her class does reading in the library. Anna keeps asking if she can sit with Carrie, but Carrie really doesn't like Anna. Carrie tells her teacher that Anna called her a bad name, just to get her in trouble.

Good Decision/Bad Decision - Scenario Cards 6-5

Ellen always sees Brian poking his pencil in Robert's back. Ellen is worried that Robert might get hurt, but he isn't telling the teacher. Ellen asks her teacher if she can talk with her in the hall.

Courtney likes to try to trip kids on the playground. Most kids think it is funny. Eric worries that someone might get hurt. Eric tells Courtney if she doesn't stop, he will tell the teacher, because someone might get hurt.

QUEST Program I Social Skills Curriculum for Elementary School Students with Autism
© by JoEllen Cumpata and Susan Fell. Future Horizons, Inc.

When I Have a Problem - Report 6-5

Names_____

Date_____

Directions: Read the sentences below. Fill in the blanks for each question. Look at the story or use the word box if you need help.

1. Kids usually feel comfortable and happy in school, but sometimes they feel angry, sad, or _____.

2. It is hard to listen, be _____, use good manners, and cooperate when you feel sad, angry, or frustrated.

3. Sometimes kids need _____ from an adult in school -principals, teachers, and classroom assistants- are all ready to help students work through problems.

4. Fighting and being disrespectful are against school _____ and can get kids in trouble.

5. Adults can help kids make good choices when they are angry, so they don't get in _____.

6. It is okay to tell an adult about _____ in school or problems with other students.

7. If you feel sad, angry, or frustrated in class, you should:

    - raise your hand;

    - ask your teacher to talk in _____;

    - tell the teacher about the problem.

8. Teachers and principals are good problem _____.

9. Teachers might talk about ways to solve the problem, _____ with other students or even make changes in the classroom like moving a student's seat.

10. Problem solving is one way teachers help kids have a fun and _____ day.

WORD BOX

respectful	private	relaxing
rules	help	solvers
problems	frustrated	talk
trouble		

QUEST Program I UPDATE!

Dear Parent,

Your child has been working hard in QUEST Program I this week to learn and practice social skills. The story we read to introduce our new skill was called:

When I Have a Problem

Together we have learned:

- Why it is important to ask adults for help with problems in school.

- The appropriate way to request help.

You can help your child practice at home by:

- Encouraging your child to seek out adult assistance when they express concerns about school-related issues.

    e.g., "That's a tough situation, Sally. I know Mrs. Green would really like to help. Could you talk with her about it tomorrow?"

- Requesting assistance from school staff when your child is unable to work through school related problems.

    e.g., "I know Jeremy may be uncomfortable bringing this up in class, but he is really having a problem with Josh. Would you chat with him about it?"

Thanks for your help!

QUEST Program I Parent/Teacher Evaluation
Unit 6 - Being Responsible

Student Name _____ Date _____

Parent/Teacher Name _____

We have just completed a unit in QUEST Program I on Personal Safety. Please fill out the rating scale below to assist us in determining how well your student has generalized the skills taught and if you have noticed improvement in their level of skill over the past six weeks. Check all boxes which apply below.

Skill	Does Independently	Does Only With Adult Reminders	Improvement Noted (Post-test only)
Being Respectful of Others: Asking before touching the personal belongings of others, using appropriate personal space.			
Using Good Manners: Listening when others are talking, waiting their turn, and says "Please" and Thank you.			
Correcting Adults: Understanding and accepting that adults may do things differently, refraining from arguing or correcting adults, following through with adult requests.			
Cooperating: Sharing materials and is able to relax, listen, and talk through disagreements.			
When I Have a Problem: Requesting assistance from adults rather than shutting down or acting out.			

Comments_____

_____

Thank you for your input!

QUEST Program I Social Skills Curriculum for Elementary School Students with Autism
© by JoEllen Cumpata and Susan Fell. Future Horizons, Inc.

Index